Divine Ladders (Part One)

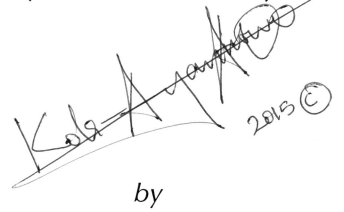

2015 ©

by

Akinwale Kola-Ayannowo

Divine Ladders (Part One)

ISBN: 978-1-909206-11-3

Published by Divine Grace Enterprises Limited.

www.divinegraceenterprise.com
Cover Design by: Zoe Communications Limited.
Printed in the United Kingdom and the United States of America.

Scripture quotations are from the New King James Version of the Bible unless otherwise indicated.

DEDICATION

0380C350

This book is dedicated to my precious Lord and Saviour Jesus Christ, who has given me and all those who believe in Him—the gift of eternal life. I'm very grateful to my Lord for inspiring me to write my fourth book, which is aimed at letting people know that there are *Divine Ladders* to climb and that the Lord is willing to help us climb, if we will co-operate with Him.

ACKNOWLEDGEMENTS

CBEDCBED

I would like to thank Our General Overseer of the Redeemed Christian Church of God. RCCG, Daddy G O. For providing leadership.

My Beloved Mother, Mrs Adelphine Abosede Ayannowo, through whom God brought me to this world, and every member of my family.

I want to strongly appreciate Pastor Femi Akingbade, our Parish Pastor at Trinity Zone of the RCCG for his personal words of encouragement as regards the completion and publishing of this good work.

I want to also say kudos to all my well-wishers that have been supportive of me in fulfilling my calling and life purpose.

I love you all and you are precious to me. Many thanks and God bless you all real good. Amen.

CONTENTS

Introduction   *vii*

CHAPTER ONE
What Ladders Stands For   *1*

CHAPTER TWO
Step-by-Step Divine Ladders from One to Twenty-Five   *7*
  1   Divine Ladder of Righteousness   7
  2   Divine Ladder of Holiness   9
  3   Divine Ladder of Obedience   12
  4   Divine Ladder of Grace   14
  5   Divine Ladder of Mercy   18
  6   Divine Ladder of Praise and Worship   20
  7   Divine Ladder of Thanksgiving   23
  8   Divine Ladder of Giving and Receiving   25
  9   Divine Ladder of Humility   28
10   Divine Ladder of Prayer   31
11   Divine Ladder of the Fear of the Lord   34
12   Divine Ladder of Compassion   37
13   Divine Ladder of the Fruit of the Spirit   39
14   Divine Ladder of Knowledge   41
15   Divine Ladder of Understanding   43
16   Divine Ladder of Wisdom   47
17   Divine Ladder of Submission   49
18   Divine Ladder of Forgiveness   54
19   Divine Ladder of Favour   57
20   Divine Ladder of Faith   59
21   Divine Ladder of Truth   60

22   Divine Ladder of Character   63
23   Divine Ladder of Sacrifice   64
24   Divine Ladder of Tithing   67
25   Divine Ladder of More and More of Jesus   70

CHAPTER THREE
Step-by-Step Divine Ladders from Twenty-Six to Fifty-Two   73
26   Divine Ladder of Service Unto the Lord   73
27   Divine Ladder of Trust in the Lord   76
28   Divine Ladder of the Overflow of the Holy Spirit   78
29   Divine Ladder of First Fruits   79
30   Divine Ladder of Comfort   81
31   Divine Ladder of Anointing   83
32   Divine Ladder of Power   86
33   Divine Ladder of Seeking God's Face   87
34   Divine Ladder of Diligence   88
35   Divine Ladder of Direction   90
36   Divine Ladder of Zeal   92
37   Divine Ladder of the Presence of the Lord   94
38   Divine Ladder of Correction   96
39   Divine Ladder of Salvation (Staying Saved in the Lord)   98
40   Divine Ladder of Exploits   100
41   Divine Ladder of Endurance   101
42   Divine Ladder of Inheritance   103
43   Divine Ladder of Encouragement   105
44   Divine Ladder of Revelation   107
45   Divine Ladder of Help   110
46   Divine Ladder of Hope   113
47   Divine Ladder of Healing   114
48   Divine Ladder of Health   118
49   Divine Ladder of Transformation of the Mind   119
50   Divine Ladder of Destiny   121
51   Divine Ladder of Exchange and Transfer   124
52   Divine Ladder of Possibilities   127

Conclusion   *130*
Other Books by the Author   *132*

INTRODUCTION

 C380C380

The word 'ladder' is not a common word that people use in their day to day conversations. This word actually appears in the entire Bible just once in (Genesis 28:12), which we will study in detail in this book. The issue of ladders came to me earlier in the year 2014 when the General Overseer of RCCG said we should embark on 100 days of fasting and prayer. During this period as I was praying and seeking God's face—the word ladders repeatedly came to me, and I kept hearing God's voice telling me to climb His given ladders. This prompted me to further investigate the word 'ladders' so that I could discover in depth what it means, and of what importance it can be to a man.

You might, for instance, be familiar with the word 'Property Ladder', which is often used in some circles to explain the fact that the earlier you get on the property ladder, the better for you. Looking at the UK for example and the way the economy has changed since the global recession in 2008—it has now become a big challenge if I may use light words for 'First Time Buyers' to purchase a house. Mortgage lenders now often require a substantial amount of deposit from first-time buyers, which wasn't the case prior to the start of the recession in 2008. The phrase 'property ladder' is not about people climbing a visual ladder, and to remain on it but, mainly an expression used to describe acquiring your own property and with the right experience of managing it, increasing the numbers of properties purchased to build your property portfolio. God helping you!

I want to thank God for those of us who bought houses before the time we are in, and I also want to believe that God wants to make a way for as many of His children who want to buy even now. Remember the Bible says in (Luke 1:37), "For with God nothing will be impossible."

My above explanation of the phrase 'property ladder' is just an example of how, for instance, the word 'ladder' is being used in the secular world for things. This same word 'ladder' also applies to spiritual matters and, this is why in (Genesis 28:10-22), the Bible gives a full account of Jacob's experience in a dream of how he saw a ladder that was set on earth and extended all the way to heaven and how the angels of the Lord were rising and descending on it; at the very top of this ladder that extended to heaven was the Lord standing above it and speaking to Jacob in this dream he was having.

What a fantastic experience this is. I want to say at this point that there are good ladders and bad ladders. People climb them for various reasons even in the natural sense, which in most cases might be to arrive at a place that is beyond the reach of the person while standing on the ground. A lot of workmen who build houses, in order for them to access certain areas that they cannot reach or see from just standing on the ground use ladders to do so. Also, in most workplaces, there are professional ladders that people have to climb in order to reach the top of their careers. I'm sure we will all agree that almost every workplace has a ladder of promotion and a hierarchy ladder, which defines who is who and who can do or authorise what. For instance, in most secular organisations the BOARD and the CEO (Chief Executive Officer) at the top of the organisation structure hierarchy are the ones responsible for making key decisions and, also for overseeing the implementation of the decisions made.

There are, of course, also several spiritual ladders that we as God's children need to know about and climb. I must say that my books on this topic are not written to paint a picture that I have exhausted everything there is to do with spiritual ladders, but I've covered to the best of my knowledge the areas that God has revealed to me. This book is titled: *Divine Ladders* because all the ladders l have explained in this book are *God Given* ladders from The Almighty God.

As I had mentioned, there are good ladders and bad ladders, natural ladders and spiritual ones but both Part one and two of my books on the topic of—divine *ladders* are mainly centred on the spiritual ones. This topic of 'divine ladders' is covered in two books to give me the room necessary to address about 100 divine ladders that we need to climb as disciples of Jesus with the help of the LORD.

1

What Ladders Stand For

ᏣᏞᏢᏣᏞᏢ

I mentioned a bit in my introduction about what ladders stand for. Collins English Dictionary defines a ladder as: "A portable framework of wood, metal, rope, etc. in the form of two long parallel members connected by several parallel rungs or steps fixed to them at right angles for climbing up or down. Any hierarchy conceived of as having a series of ascending stages, levels, etc. the social ladder."

A ladder can also be seen as a means to rise to popularity or eminence. From the above definition—we can see that as an individual starts to climb a ladder be it a physical or a spiritual one, they begin to rise above others and others have to look up to them for direction or guidance. Ladders can be said to be the media by, which we climb up from one point to another. My focus in this book is to look at climbing upwards spiritually and not downwards. I want to use this writing to encourage Christians that they have God-given ladders to climb and that it is up to us to co-operate with the Holy Spirit (Our Helper) to do so.

I want to add that the climbing of ladders in this book should be seen as us maturing, increasing, being established, growing and ever increasing spiritually in all areas of our Christian lives with the help of the Holy Spirit because by ourselves we can do nothing.

"I am the vine, you are the branches. He who abides in Me, and I in him, bears much fruit; for without Me you can do nothing" (John 15:5).

To begin with let us take a closer look at Jacob's dream and what it means. The Bible in Genesis 28:10-17 says:

"Now Jacob went out from Beersheba and went toward Haran. So he came to a certain place and stayed there all night because the sun had set. And he took one of the stones of that place and put it at his head, and he lay down in that place to sleep. Then he dreamed and behold a ladder was set up on earth, and its top reached to heaven and there the angels of God were ascending and descending on it. And behold, the LORD stood above it and said: "I am the LORD God of Abraham your father and the God of Isaac, the land on which you lie I will give to you and your descendants.

Also your descendants shall be as the dust of the earth, you shall spread abroad to the west and the east, to the north and the south and in you and your seed all the families of the earth shall be blessed. Behold, I am with you and will keep you wherever you go, and will bring you back to this land, for I will not leave you until I have done what I have spoken to you."

Then Jacob awoke from his sleep and said, "Surely the LORD is in this place, and I did not know it." And he was afraid and said, 'How awesome is this place! This is none other than the house of God, and this is the gate of heaven!"

The encounter that Jacob had in this dream is one which can be looked at from various perspectives. I want to point out the following:

1. **The ladder that Jacob saw in his dream was set from the earth and its top reached to heaven:** I'm sure no man in his natural thinking can imagine a ladder like this. This points to the fact that it is not a natural ladder, but a spiritual one for step-by-step climbing in the realms of the spirit. This ladder also starts with the Lord and ends with Him.

2. **Only Jacob saw this ladder from earth:** This shows that the issue of climbing spiritual ladders is a personal thing and I believe that all of God's children have to believe Him for their own God-given ladders to climb, so that we are not in competition with one another or at rivalry. The Bible in John (14:1-3), says:

   "Let not your heart be troubled; you believe in God, believe also in Me. In My Father's house are many mansions; if it were not so, I would have told you. I go to prepare a place for you, I will come again and receive you to Myself, that where I am, there you may be also".

Jesus used the word many mansions and I believe there are more than enough of them in heaven for all of God's children, we will each have ours. We will not be arguing or struggling over space or mansions and I believe that it's the same principle here on earth. Our Father in heaven owns the whole heaven and the earth—each and every one of us have our own allotted portion both here on earth and in heaven. I'm sure we would agree that as God's children we have His Holy Spirit in us all. Therefore we are also carrying His anointing and we are at different depths and levels of that anointing. The same thing applies to the issue of God given ladders. Each and every one of us have our own God-given ladders to climb so there is no need to envy any one at all. It's now up to you and me with the help of the Holy Spirit to climb and make a difference in this world to the glory of His name.

3. **Angels ascending and descending on the ladder:** In verses 12 of Genesis Chapter 28's account of Jacob's dream, we see that angels were ascending and descending on the ladder that Jacob saw. This could be for the purpose of taking things from Jacob up to the LORD and bringing things down to him from the LORD. One conclusion I have made in regards to my own God-given spiritual ladders is, that I just want to keep climbing higher and higher, and to keep taking hold of

all that God has for me in the name of Jesus. Remember the climbing is a spiritual climb and not a physical one. In case you are wondering how this can be possible, the Bible in (John 17:11-13), says:

> "Now I am no longer in the world, but these are in the world, and I come to You. Holy Father, keep through Your name those whom You have given Me, that they may be one as We are. While I was with them in the world, I kept them in Your name. Those whom You gave Me I have kept; and none of them is lost except the son of perdition, that the Scripture might be fulfilled. But now I come to You, and these things I speak in the world, that they may have My joy fulfilled in themselves".

We can see from the words of Jesus, that even though He was praying for His disciples on earth He says, in verse 11: "Now I am no longer in the world…….," even though Jesus was saying these prayers, while He was still physically in the world because He hadn't gone to the cross yet to die for mankind.

In verse 13 Jesus says: "But now I come to You, and these things I speak in the world…" which, suggests that Jesus was still in the world, yet to go to be with the Father in heaven. The point I'm trying to make from these verses of the Scripture is that a disciple of Jesus can mature to a position where he or she is on earth yet live as if in heaven. There is a total connection with heaven that even though the person is physically on earth, it can be said that he/she is also in heaven because of that bond with heaven. This makes it possible to be on earth physically, while in the realm of the spirit, one is climbing spiritual ladders up to heaven. We can also in the realm of the spirit ascend all our God-given spiritual ladders because on earth as human beings, we play different roles every single day of our lives. For example; you can be an Engineer by profession at work, a husband and a father at home, a pastor or a teacher at church, etc.

4. **The ladder extended from the earth to heaven:** In verses 13 of Genesis 28, we see that the Lord stood above the ladder that extended from the earth to heaven, and in the dream Jacob heard the Lord talk to him, by introducing Himself first, then blessing him and telling him things about his future. I would like to say that as we climb our God-given ladders that extend from the earth to heaven on a daily basis–we will be drawing closer and closer to the Lord, which I'm sure all God's children will desire. I need to emphasize once more that the issue of climbing God-given ladders should be seen as us maturing, increasing, enlarging and being established daily in the Lord, for which there is no end until we meet with Jesus face to face.

It is a call to an ever increasing and ever-maturing in the Lord Jesus, till we meet with Him either through falling asleep from the earth or in the rapture. This is signified by the ladder Jacob saw starting from earth and extending all the way to heaven.

2

Step-by-Step Divine Ladders from One to Twenty-Five

ෆ෨෬෨

1
Divine Ladder of Righteousness

The words righteousness and righteous appear in the Bible 315 and 262 times respectively (NKJV). The first man to be called righteous in the Bible was Noah in (Genesis 7:1):

> 'Then the LORD said to Noah "Come into the ark, you and all your household, because I have seen that you are righteous before Me in this generation".

The word righteous can mean morally right or justifiable when someone is acting in an upright manner before God. It can be said to mean someone standing right and doing what is right in the sight of the Almighty God. Righteousness is more about action, which starts with accepting Jesus Christ as Lord and Saviour. The Bible in (Philippians 3: 9), says:

> "And being found in Him, not having my own righteousness, which is from the law, but that which is through faith in Christ, the righteousness which is from God by faith".

God expects us as His children to walk right before Him always. I'm not talking here about self-righteousness, but about the righteousness that we have grace to achieve with the help of the Holy Spirit. This is to say that as we have been called by His grace we need to step-by-step climb the divine ladder of Righteousness, which started with us accepting Jesus Christ as our personal Lord and Saviour to remain right with God. We can develop on this through the study of the Word and doing exactly what the Bible, which is the mind of God reveals to us and expects us to do.

The people who are law-abiding citizens of a country, for instance, tend to study the law of the country and stay on the right side of it in order not to offend. As children of God, we can do exactly the same with Him, by diligently studying His word, and doing exactly what it says to remain right with the Almighty God. And, as we do this daily, we will step-by-step be climbing the divine ladder of righteousness. I noted from studying the Bible that, God always rewards righteousness. The below Bible verses are evidence of this:

> "For You, O LORD, will bless the righteous; With favour You will surround him as with a shield" (Psalm 5:12).

"The righteous is delivered from trouble, And it comes to the wicked instead." (Proverbs 11:8).

I must say that our righteousness is in Christ Jesus and we live righteous before God by responding to His grace with the help of the Holy Spirit our Helper. So, as we co-operate with the Holy Spirit of God in us as His children, we are able to live right before Him and on a daily basis step-by-step climb the ladder of righteousness, which we started by accepting Jesus as our Lord and Saviour. Not responding to God's grace and the help of the Holy Spirit, makes it difficult to live right before Him. Matthew Chapter 5 verses 6 says:

"Blessed are those who hunger and thirst for righteousness, for they shall be filled."

Our hunger and thirst for God's righteousness, can be done by our step-by-step climbing the divine ladder of righteousness with the help of the Holy Spirit.

2
Divine Ladder of Holiness
❊❧❦❊❊❧❦❊

The word 'holiness' is featured in the Bible 32 times, while the word 'holy' is featured 637 times. What does it mean to be holy? It simply means for you and I to separate ourselves aside for God's use and purpose; to be set aside unto God. It means to reserve ourselves exclusively for the Almighty God and nothing and nobody else. It means to be clean and pure before God. Our holiness before Him is about all we are doing, saying, watching, thinking, imagining and so on, leading us to the condition of being separated and uncontaminated unto God. For example, if you have a glass of purified water, the moment that you pour orange juice into it, it is no longer purified water.

God said in (Leviticus 11:45):

> "For I am the LORD who brings you up out of the land of Egypt, to be your God. You shall therefore be holy for I am holy."

This means that the Almighty God is pure, completely perfect and separate from all sin. Our God is far above all moral imperfections and setbacks associated with mankind. Holiness is God's nature and this is why the Bible in Daniel 4:8-9 says:

> "But at last Daniel came before me (his name *is* Belteshazzar, according to the name of my god; in him *is* the Spirit of the Holy God), and I told the dream before him, *saying*: Belteshazzar chief of the magicians, because I know that the Spirit of the Holy God *is* in you, and no secret troubles you, explain to me the visions of my dream that I have seen, and its interpretation."

So the Almighty God is The Holy God, He is the One and Only Holy God.

Isaiah 40:25 also says:

> "To whom then will you liken Me, Or to whom shall I be equal? Says the Holy One"

The Almighty God is called "The Holy One Of Israel" in the Bible 29 times. One of such Scriptures, which I love so much is Isaiah 41:14 which says:

> "Fear not, you worm Jacob You men of Israel! I will help you," says the LORD And your Redeemer, the Holy One of Israel."

This is why the Bible says in Exodus 19:6 that:

> "And you shall be to Me a kingdom of priest and a holy nation.' These are the words which you shall speak to the children of Israel."

We see The Holy God calling the nation of Israel to separate itself unto Him. Also, 1 Peter 2:9 says:

> "But you are a chosen generation, a royal priesthood, a holy nation, His own special people, that you may proclaim the praises of Him who called you out of darkness into His marvellous light."

Our separation and setting apart unto The Holy God after we have given our lives to Jesus Christ marks the beginning of our walk in holiness with the LORD, hence we start with the help of the Holy Spirit, to step-by-step climb the divine ladder of holiness. I must say that there are different levels of holiness; this we can confirm in the Bible in Exodus 26:33:

> "And you shall hang the veil from the clasps. Then you shall bring the ark of the Testimony in there, behind the veil. The veil shall be a divider for you between the holy place and the Most Holy."

So as we start to climb the divine ladder of holiness, we move from one level of holiness to another unto the LORD with the help of the Holy Spirit and our own co-operation. And as we do this, The Holy God will continue to delight in us and we will be pleasing in His sight. There is a divine ladder of holiness to climb, in order for us to be holy in spirit, soul and body. One thing this will do for us is that we will have no pleasure in sin and will start to work on maturity and perfection unto the Lord. Also, our thoughts will not be ruled and guided by culture or tradition but by the Word of God only. I pray this for you and me in the name of Jesus. Amen!

3
Divine Ladder of Obedience
✵⚭⚮✵⚭✵⚭⚮✵

The word obedience and obey appeared in the Bible 14 and 108 times respectively. We see throughout the Bible, God speaking to us, His children, to obey Him and be blessed. Deuteronomy 28:1-15 highlights blessings for obedience and verses 15-68 highlights curses for disobedience. My prayer is that we will be obedient children before God so that we can be blessed in the name of Jesus.

To obey God means to comply and to follow God based on His word. This is to say that we live the Bible and follow God's instructions always, whether they suit us or not; whether we agree with them or not. If it is written in the Bible, God expects us to obey it. There is a divine ladder of obedience that God's children need to climb with the Help of the Holy Spirit and by His Grace. We also need to play our part by willingly yielding our will to God's will through obedience.

From my little experience, obeying God gets easier when we make up our minds as His children to willingly surrender our will to His will. God is not going to force us, and people at times struggle to obey God because they don't want to surrender their own will to God's own. There is nothing one can give to replace obedience to God. This is why the Bible says in (1 Samuel 15: 22-23), that:

> "So Samuel said: Has the LORD as great delight in burnt offerings and sacrifices, As in obeying the voice of the LORD? Behold, to obey is better than sacrifice, And to heed than the fat of rams. For rebellion is as the sin of witchcraft, And stubbornness is as iniquity and idolatry. Because you have rejected the word of the LORD, He also has rejected you from being king."

The story of King Saul is a common story for us as Christians to learn from. As we see in the Bible, King Saul was rejected by God because of his disobedience to God's word. As we obey God on a daily basis we are step-by-step climbing-unknown to us-the divine ladder of obedience, which will definitely lead to God's blessings. Job 36:11 says:

> "If they obey and serve Him, They shall spend their days in prosperity, And their years in pleasures."

As we climb the divine ladder of obedience on a daily basis, we will continue to please the Almighty God and find pleasure in His sight and be blessed by Him.

4
Divine Ladder of Grace
✳❦❧❀❦❧✳

A lot of people will accept that the Almighty God is a gracious God. The grace that God has made available to mankind is at different levels. The word grace appears in the Bible 148 times. God's grace can be defined as His free and undeserved acts of goodness, kindness and favour towards mankind. God's general grace has been made available to the whole of mankind through the death of Jesus Christ on the cross. This grace is even available to those who are yet to be born into planet earth.

Titus 2:11-12 says:

> "For the grace of God that brings salvation has appeared to all men, teaching us that, denying ungodliness and worldly lust, we should live soberly, righteously, and godly in the present age."

Here we can see that even though God's grace is available to all individually. We need to respond to it and do certain things with the help of the Holy Spirit as a sign that we haven't taken God's grace for granted. Man's proper response to God's saving grace of salvation puts him (man) in a place where he can be moved further and deeper into accessing higher levels of grace. This is what I mean by climbing the divine ladder of grace. Not responding to God's saving grace of salvation through Jesus Christ will limit man's access to higher levels of grace in God.

Climbing the ladder of God's grace puts us in a place where we can grow from grace to grace. Let's look at what the Bible says about different levels of God's grace:

> "For if by the one man's offense death reigned through the one, much more those who received abundance of grace and of the gift of righteousness will reign in life through the One, Jesus Christ" (Romans 5:17).

Here we see that there is abundance of grace for those who have responded to Jesus Christ and accepted Him as LORD and SAVIOUR.

"And with great power the apostles gave witness to the resurrection of the Lord Jesus. And great grace was upon them all" (Acts 4:33).

Here the 'them all' is referring to the apostles operating under God's great grace, which is a higher dimension of God's grace. This is not general grace for everyone.

"Even so then, at this present time there is a remnant according to the election of grace" (Romans 11:5)

This verse of Scripture makes us realise that God choses certain people at times to show special kindness and favour. A very good example I will say is the choosing of Abraham out of the heathen.

"And God is able to make all grace abound toward you that you, always having all sufficiency in all things, may have an abundance for every good work" (2 Corinthians 9:8).

"But to each one of us grace was given according to the measure of Christ's gift." Verse 11 of the same chapter says: "And He Himself gave some to be apostles, some prophets, some evangelist, and some pastors and teachers" (Ephesians 4:7).

This is talking about different levels of grace that have been made available to us to operate in a variety of offices and levels in ministry. The story of talents in (Matthew 25:14-30), also confirms different levels of grace.

> "But He gives more grace. Therefore, He says: "God resists the proud But gives grace to the humble" (James 4:6).

Here we are told of more grace available to the humble and not the proud.

> "You therefore, beloved, since you know this beforehand, beware lest you also fall from your own steadfastness, being led away with the error of the wicked; but grow in the grace and knowledge of our Lord and Saviour Jesus Christ. To Him be the glory both now and forever. Amen" (2 Peter 3:17-18).

Here we see that there is the growing in grace from one level to another when we co-operate with God. This is what I mean by step-by-step climbing of the divine ladder of grace and not remaining at the elementary levels of it.

I must emphasise at this point that with all that I have mentioned so far on the issue of grace, the one important thing we must always bear in mind is that, God's grace for us as revealed in the entire Bible context, is not a license for us to continuing sinning and displeasing God. Sin can only lead to separation from God and if our desire is to remain connected with Him, we must abstain from sin altogether. I pray that the LORD will help us to do so daily in Jesus mighty name.

"What then? Shall we sin because we are not under law but grace? Certainly not! Do you not know that to whom you present yourselves slaves to obey, you are that one's slaves whom you obey, whether of sin leading to death or of obedience leading to righteousness?" (Romans 6:15-16).

"Let grace be shown to the wicked, Yet he will not learn righteousness; In the land of uprightness he will deal unjustly, And will not behold the majesty of the LORD" (Isaiah 26:10).

"For certain men have crept in unnoticed, who long ago were marked out for this condemnation, ungodly men, who turned the grace of our God into lewdness and deny the only Lord God and our Lord Jesus Christ" (Jude 1:4).

These three Scriptures show us that, the fact that God's grace is available unto all doesn't mean that man is free to do whatever he wishes. With grace also comes accountability. I pray that all my readers will start to climb higher and higher on the divine ladder of grace as you read this book in the name of Jesus.

5
Divine Ladder of Mercy
ℋℰℰℰℰℰℰℋ

The word 'mercy' is featured in the Bible 282 times, God's mercy can be said to mean God not giving us the punishment we deserve for our wrong doing. Two Scriptures in the book of Romans makes it clear to us that we all have offended God, but God decided not to give us the punishment deserved but to show us mercy.

"For all have sinned and fall short of the glory of God" (Romans 3:23).

"For the wages of sin is death, but the gift of God is eternal life in Christ Jesus our Lord" (Romans 6:23).

We can see from the two verses above in the book of Romans, that salvation came to us as a result of God's mercy to mankind not that we merited or did something about it. Instead of handing out the death penalty, God chose in His mercy to hand out life to as many as will receive it. Instead of allowing us to perish permanently in wages of our sins, God placed the consequences of sins, which is death on Jesus for the remission of our sins, to ensure that we become saved and redeemed from judgement of sins when we repent and receive Him into our lives to be our personal Lord and Saviour.

"What shall we say then? Is there unrighteousness with God? Certainly not! For he says to Moses, "I will have mercy on whomever I will have mercy, and compassion on whomever I will have compassion." So then it is not of him who wills, nor of him who runs, but of God who shows mercy. For the scripture says to the Pharaoh, "For this very purpose I have raised you up, that I may show My power in you, and that My name may be declared in all the earth. Therefore He has mercy on whom he wills, and whom He wills He hardens" (Romans 9:14-18)

There is a God-given ladder of mercy that we can climb step-by-step, so that the abundant mercy of God will always be available to us in times of need. As we climb higher and higher on this God-given ladder, I believe the Almighty God will continue to pour out His unlimited mercy upon us in the name of Jesus.

Isaiah 54:10 says: "For the mountains shall depart And the hills be removed, But My kindness shall not depart from you, Nor shall My covenant of peace be removed," Says the LORD, who has mercy on you."

The kindness of God not departing and the covenant of peace not being removed by the Almighty God are both as a result of His mercies upon us. Alleluia!

6
Divine Ladder of Praise and Worship

Here I am talking about praising and worshipping the Almighty God our Lord and Maker. To praise God means to give thanks, to confess, to honour, to pay homage or admiration to Him. It also means to proclaim His wonders and goodness towards us and humanity. To worship God means to reverence and honour Him for who He is. It is a spiritual act to the Almighty God with full focus on Him for who He is and not what He has done. This act of worship must be in spirit and in truth.

The word 'praise' is in the Bible 237 times whilst the word 'worship' appears 112 times. The main difference between praise and worship is that, in praise we are exalting and thanking God for what He has done, what He is doing and what we are believing Him to do in the near future, whereas worship, is all about reverencing and honouring God for who He is. For example praise is saying: 'Lord I praise you for helping me today to overcome all my challenges at work', and worship is saying: 'Lord I bless you because You are the Almighty God, my God I AM THAT I AM, You are the Omnipotent, Omniscient and Omnipresent God.' There is a divine ladder of praise and worship that God's children need to climb step-by-step every day in order to please Him.

> Psalm 150:6 says: "Let everything that has breath praise the Lord. Praise the LORD."

It might interest you to know that the word praise appears 152 times out of the whole 237 times in the Bible in the book of Psalms written by David. This is not surprising because the Almighty God calls David, a man after His own heart.

21

"And when He had removed him, He raised up for them David as king, to whom also He gave testimony and said, 'I have found David the son of Jesse, a man after My own heart, who will do all My will'" (Acts 13:22).

Let's remind ourselves also of what God did in (2 Chronicles 20:22),

"Now when they began to sing and to praise, the LORD set ambushes against the people of Ammon, Moab, and Mount Seir, who had come against Judah; and they were defeated."

This is what praise and worship of God can do for us His children.

"Give unto the LORD the glory due to His name; Worship the LORD in the beauty of holiness. The voice of the LORD is over the waters; The God of glory thunders; The LORD is over many waters. The voice of the LORD is powerful; The voice of the LORD is full of majesty" (Psalm 29:2-4).

We can praise and worship God in various ways; in our words, our dance, with instruments and in songs. We can also praise and worship God standing up, sitting down or lying down. Our praise and worship of Him will always bring down

His presence to help us. We should endeavour to praise and worship God always.

7
Divine Ladder of Thanksgiving

The word thanksgiving simply means to give thanks; to God Almighty for what He has done, for what He is yet to do for all things and always. There is a divine ladder of thanksgiving that God's children need to climb daily in appreciation to Him always. The word 'thanksgiving' is featured in the Bible 32 times, the word 'give thanks' 40 times, the word 'thanks' appears 75 times and the word 'thank you' appears in the Bible 7 times.

> "In everything give thanks; for this is the will of God in Christ Jesus for you" (1 Thessalonians 5:18).

We are encouraged to give thanks to God always both in good and challenging times because God will be pleased with us as we do this. We are also through this act putting ourselves in a place where He can bless us and show us His goodness. I'm sure you would agree that even as human beings we tend to appreciate, people who show gratitude more than those who don't.

> "But we are bound to give thanks to God always for you, brethren beloved by the Lord, because God from the

beginning chose you for salvation through sanctification by the Spirit and belief in the truth" (2 Thessalonians 2:13).

We can see from this Scripture that we are all bound to give thanks to God always, for the salvation of our spirits and souls in Christ Jesus.

"Oh that men would give thanks to the LORD for His goodness and wonderful works to the children of men! For He has broken the gates of bronze, And cut the bars of iron in two" (Psalm 107:15-16).

"Then He took the cup and gave thanks, and said, "Take this and divide it among yourselves" (Luke 22:17).

This Scripture is talking about our Lord Jesus who also gave thanks to our Father in heaven and, since we are called to be like Jesus, we also need to do the same always.

There is a divine ladder of thanksgiving that we need to climb always, in order to give God glory. We also need to say thank you to the people around us, who have rendered some form of help and goodwill to us as a sign of appreciation. Not giving thanks to God Almighty is a sign of wickedness. I pray we all will continue to step-by-step climb higher and higher on this divine ladder of thanksgiving in the name of Jesus. Amen.

8
Divine Ladder of Giving and Receiving
ℋ❧✦◐❧✦ℋ

In case you are wondering why I'm looking at giving and receiving as joint one divine ladder to climb, I would like to explain by saying, it is because they go hand in hand, and the only way to keep receiving is to keep giving. If you are not fed up of receiving from God, then you can't be fed up of giving. I personally see my right leg as my giving leg and my left leg as my receiving and the only way to walk or move forward is to move one leg after the other. It's not possible to keep moving one without moving the other, and I don't think it would be possible to walk unless those movements are sequential

A simple definition for the word 'give' is to hand something over from your heart willingly and cheerfully. And a definition for 'receive', is to accept something into your possession. These two words can be defined from various perspectives, but I want to look at the two words mainly from the context of giving and receiving between man to man, God to man and man to God.

The word 'give' appears in the Bible 865 times whereas the word 'receive' appears 173 times. This is not a surprise because the Bible says in (Acts 20:35), that:

> "I have shown you in every way by labouring like this, that you must support the weak. And remember the words

of the Lord Jesus that He said 'It is more blessed to give than to receive.'"

All throughout the Bible we see the Almighty God as a giving God and that He is also a receiving God; also that man is a giver and a receiver, which makes us like God. There is definitely a divine ladder of giving and receiving for me and you ordained by God, which we can climb step-by-step on a daily basis. There is no end to our giving and receiving from God's perspective. Remember that before you and I ever gave anything to God at all, He had given so much to us first. Right from the book of Genesis, He (God) made man in His own image, giving us His identity. He also gave man all good things to enjoy after creation in the book of Genesis. Out of all God's giving throughout the Bible I want to show you just two very important acts of God's giving:

> "So God created man in His own image, in the image of God He created him, male and female He created them. Then God blessed them, and God said to them, "Be fruitful and multiply, fill the earth and subdue it; have dominion over the fish of the sea, over the birds of the air, and over every living thing that moves on the earth" (Genesis 1:27-28).

From this Scripture, we can see that not only did God create man by giving him life, He also gave man what I call the ability to be like God in all areas of his existence. John 3:16 says:

> "For God so loved the world that He gave His only begotten Son, that whoever believes in Him should not perish but have everlasting life."

From giving us, Christ Jesus, we see God giving His very best for the saving of fallen man. So, as God has given to us, it is only appropriate that we give back to Him our lives, our worship and praise, our substance, our time and so on. All throughout the Bible we read of God giving one thing or the other to man so we also ought to give back to him:

> "Give, and it will be given to you: good measure, pressed down, shaken together, and running over will be put into your bosom. For with the same measure that you use, it will be measured back to you" (Luke 6:38).

We are also encouraged in various places in the Bible to give to fellow man for instance in the following verses in the book of Proverbs:

> "He who has pity on the poor lends to the LORD, And He will pay back what he has given" (Proverbs 19:17).

> "He who gives to the poor will not lack, But he who hides his eyes will have many curses" (Proverbs 27:27).

Not only are we to give to the needy but we can also give to other people for various reasons, for example giving a gift of appreciation and love to someone. There is a divine ladder of giving and receiving to climb on a daily basis. I personally see the issue of giving and receiving as important as breathing oxygen in order to stay alive. The things we can give include time, service, advice, help and support, money, gifts, words of encouragement just to mention a few.

9
Divine Ladder of Humility
❈❦➷❧❀❧➷❦❈

This is a very important ladder that I believe a very high percentage of God's children seem to have ignored. The word humility simply means to be humble, to have a modest opinion of self. The word humble appears in the Bible 43 times and it reminds me of my Lord and Saviour Jesus Christ and some characters in the Bible like Joseph and Moses.

Let us remind ourselves what the Bible says about Jesus Christ and Moses in regards to humility.

> "And being found in appearance as a man, He humbled Himself and became obedient to the point of death, even the death of the cross. Therefore God also has highly exalted Him and given Him the name which is above every name, that at the name of Jesus every knee should

bow, of those in heaven, and of those on earth, and of those under the earth, and that every tongue should confess that Jesus Christ is Lord, to the glory of God the Father" (Philippians 2:8-11).

"Now the man Moses was very humble, more than all men who were on the face of the earth" (Numbers 12:3).

In this Scripture, we see Moses as a type of Jesus in humility. This I believe was the main reason why God gave Moses the great task of bringing the Israelites out of Egypt. Even after he offended God and it was time for him to leave the scene, no man buried him but God did by Himself, as a gesture of honour to Moses.

"So Moses the servant of the Lord died there in the land of Moab, according to the word of the LORD. And He buried him in a valley in the land of Moab, opposite Beth Peor: but no one knows his grave to this day" (Deuteronomy 34:5-6).

This is the kind of honour God can bestow on a humble person. The elevation of our Lord and Saviour as a result of His humility is unique and so also is that of Moses as a result of his humility because the Bible does not record for us about God Himself burying another man by Himself. If our intention is to climb step-by-step higher with God, the only way for us to achieve this is to climb the divine ladder of humility before

God and man on a daily basis. Remember also Joseph, who had the spirit of humility. With humility, we will achieve tremendous success before God and man.

> "Likewise you younger people, submit yourselves to your elders. Yes, all of you be submissive to one another and be clothed with humility, for God resists the proud, But gives grace to the humble. Therefore humble yourselves under the mighty hand of God, that He may exalt you in due time" (1 Peter 5: 5-6).

We need to understand that these Scriptures are written for people within the church to apply to their daily lives. It is unlikely to make sense to those that are yet to come to Christ and are still in the world that God's way of exaltation is through humility. My advice for anyone desiring to be great in God's kingdom is to first work on humility.

Also remember what happened to king Uzziah who became proud because of the success which God had given him:

> "But when he was strong his heart was lifted up, to his own destruction, for he transgressed against the LORD his God by entering the temple of the LORD to burn incense on the altar of incense. So Azariah the priest went in after him, and with him eighty priest of the LORD—valiant men. And they withstood King Uzziah, and said to him 'it is not for you, Uzziah to burn incense to the LORD, but for the priest, the sons of Aaron, who are consecrated

to burn incense. Get out of the sanctuary, for you have trespassed! You shall have no honour from the LORD God.' Then Uzziah became furious, and he had a censer in his hand to burn incense. And while he was angry with the priest, leprosy broke out on his forehead, before the priest in the house of the LORD, beside the incense altar.

And Azariah the chief priest and all the priest looked at him, and there, on his forehead, he was leprous; so they thrust him out of that place. Indeed he also hurried to get out, because the LORD had struck him. King Uzziah was a leper until the day of his death. He dwelt in an isolated house because he was a leper; for he was cut off from the house of the LORD." – 2 Chronicles 26:16-21a

Here we see a very successful king ending up as a leper and being separated from God and His people till his death. We need to be watchful so that pride, which God dislikes doesn't separate us from Him. The best way to do this is to climb the divine ladder of humility daily before the LORD.

10
Divine Ladder of Prayer
✄❧❦❧✄

Prayer simply means; to communicate with God. The word 'prayer' appears in the Bible 113 times whereas the word 'pray' appears 146 times. Throughout the Bible men and women prayed unto God. Even Our Lord and Saviour Jesus Christ while on earth prayed to Our Father in heaven.

> "And when He had sent them away, He departed to the mountain to pray" (Mark 6:46).

> "Now it came to pass, about eight days after these sayings, that He took Peter, John, and James and went up on the mountain to pray" (Luke 9:28)

> "Now it came to pass, as He was praying in a certain place, when He ceased, that one of His disciples said to Him, 'Lord, teach us to pray, as John also taught his disciples." So He said to them, "When you pray, say: Our Father in heaven, Hallowed be Your name. Your kingdom come. Your will be done on earth as it is in heaven. Give us day by day our daily bread. And forgive us our sins, For we also forgive everyone who is indebted to us. And do not lead us into temptation, but deliver us from the evil one" (Luke 11:1-4).

> "I pray for them. I do not pray for the world but for those whom You have given Me, for they are Yours" (John 17:9-10).

I have chosen the above four different Scriptures from the Bible to show various involvement of Jesus in prayer. In the first

Scripture, He prayed alone. In the second, He prayed with some of His disciples, which would give them an opportunity to hear and learn from Jesus how to pray. In the third Scripture, He prayed also teaching His disciples how to pray upon their request for Him to teach them how to pray. In the fourth Scripture, He prayed for all His disciples including everyone of us that is born again.

We can see that Jesus lived a life of prayer and I believe we also ought to do so. As we pray and keep praying always, what we are doing is climbing the divine ladder of prayer step-by-step.

> Luke 18:1: "Then He spoke a parable to them, that men always ought to pray and not to lose heart." (NKJV). The New Living Translations (NLT) says:

> "One day Jesus told His disciples a story to illustrate their need for constant prayer and to show them that they must never give up."

Dear reader, please never give up praying like Jesus said. Even if you are not getting the answer immediately, just keep praying and don't give up. I would also advise a prayer of thanksgiving on a constant basis too.

We need to also believe that as we climb this divine ladder of prayer step-by-step, not only is the Lord Jesus seeing us, but He is hearing us also. As long as we are praying according to His will, answers will come in the name of Jesus. Amen.

I need to say also that some of the ways in, which we can learn to pray is to listen to other Christians when they pray, and learn how to pray directly from the Bible when we read it and we see how other people prayed to God. May the Lord hear you as you climb your God given ladder of prayer in the name of Jesus. Amen.

11
Divine Ladder of the Fear of the Lord
✕⌖⌖✕⌖⌖✕

The term 'Fear of the Lord' appears in the Bible 27 times. It simply means; to respect, reverence or be in awe of the Almighty God. The fear of God is to be viewed as good for us because it puts us in a place where we want to do everything possible to please our Maker and Creator. Even in the ordinary as human beings, we tend not to want to fall out with people we have respect for.

> "The fear of the LORD is the beginning of wisdom; A good understanding have all those who do His commandments. His praise endures forever" (Psalm 111:10).

> "The fear of the LORD leads to life, And he who has it will abide in satisfaction; He will not be visited with evil" (Proverbs 19:23).

> We can see that having the fear of God in our heart, which I also call holy fear keeps us away from evil and death.

"By humility and the fear of the LORD Are riches and honour and life." (Proverbs 22:4).

If we want riches, honour and life God's way, we need to fear the Lord and please Him.

"Then the churches throughout all Judea, Galilee and Samaria had peace and were edified. And walking in the fear of the Lord and in the comfort of the Holy Spirit, they were multiplied" (Acts 9:31).

We have been called by God to live our lives in the fear of the Lord, so that He can approve of us. Remember the Almighty God owns our lives and we need to please and live for Him alone. As we step-by-step with the help of the Holy Spirit climb the divine ladder of the fear of the Lord, we will attract God's goodness and favour towards ourselves.

If you can remember, the first main reason why Joseph refused Potiphar's wife's request to lie with her was because he didn't want to sin against the Almighty God:

"But he refused and said to his master's wife, 'Look, my master does not know what is with me in the house, and he has committed all that he has to my hand. There is no one greater in this house than I, nor has he kept back anything from me but you, because you are his wife. How then can I do this great wickedness, and sin against God?" – Genesis 39:8-9

I want to believe that if Joseph had committed sin with Potiphar's wife there is the possibility that it might have affected him later on. Even though Joseph was put in prison because of lies spoken against him by Potiphar's wife, God saw him through to the top. I also want to emphasise, that we need not be afraid of human threats because the people who make them are in positions of authority. In the society we live in today, abuse of power to force people to do things which are wrong is on the increase everywhere, even in the house of God. There is grace from God to say NO in the fear of God to any man, in order to please God. And I believe that the Lord will defend such individuals.

Remember the story of Daniel in the lion's den? Also, in (Daniel 6:10-23), we see how Daniel refused to stop his regular prayers unto God despite the written decree that nobody should petition any god or man for thirty days except King Darius. He continued in his regular prayers against the signed written decree of the Medes and Persians, which does not alter. He was thrown into the lion's den for this, but God delivered him because he (Daniel) lived in the fear of God and would rather please God than man despite the threats to his natural life by man. Luke 12:4-5 says:

> "And I say to you, My friends, do not be afraid of those who kill the body, and after that have no more that they can do. But I will show you whom you should fear; Fear Him who, after He has killed, has power to cast into hell; yes I say to you, fear Him!"

As we step-by-step climb the divine ladder of the fear of the Lord on a daily basis we are drawn closer and closer to the Almighty God.

12
Divine Ladder of Compassion
❋☙❧〗❂〘☙❧❋

The word compassion appears in the Bible 47 times. It simply means; to be concerned about others, to be tenderhearted, to feel sympathy, to be moved by the suffering of others, which might not necessarily be their fault; to have pity. The word compassion is different from mercy because the word mercy is to do with God not giving us the punishment that we deserved for wrongdoing, while in the case of compassion there may or may not be any wrong doing at all. Let's look at Scriptures to confirm this:

> "But He, being full of compassion, forgave their iniquity, And did not destroy them. Yes, many a time He turned His anger away And did not stir up all His wrath" (Psalm 78:38).

Here we can see that compassion from God is as a result of wrongdoing.

Mark 8:1-3 says:

> "In those days, the multitude being very great and having nothing to eat, Jesus called His disciples to Him and said

to them "I have compassion on the multitude because they have now continued with Me three days and have nothing to eat. And if I send them away hungry to their homes they will faint on the way; for some of them have come from afar".

Then His disciples answered him, "How can one satisfy these people with bread here in the wilderness?" He asked them, "How many loaves do you have?" And they said, 'Seven' So He commanded the multitude to sit down on the ground, And He took the seven loaves and gave thanks, broke them and gave them to His disciples to set before them, and they set them before the multitude.

They also had a few small fish; and having blessed them, He said to set them also before them. So they ate and were filled, and they took up seven large baskets of leftover fragments. Now those who had eaten were about four thousand. And He sent them away."

We can see in this Scripture, Jesus showing compassion to the people, not because of sin, but because he didn't want them to go away hungry on their journey back home, which would have made life difficult, and perhaps unbearable for them since they had already been with Him three days with no food to eat.

There is a divine ladder of compassion that we need to climb so that God can continue to have compassion on us in times of hardships and sufferings. I must also emphasise that we also need to show compassion to people around us. This proves that we are God's children and have His attributes in us. 1 Peter 3:8-10 says:

> "Finally, all of you be of one mind, having compassion for one another, love as brothers, be tender hearted, be courteous; not returning evil for evil or reviling for reviling, but on the contrary blessing, knowing that you were called to this, that you may inherit a blessing."

As we climb step-by-step upwards on the divine ladder of compassion of God, we should reflect this by showing compassion towards one another.

13
Divine Ladder of the Fruit of the Spirit

Galatians 5:16 says:

> "I say then: Walk in the Spirit, and you shall not fulfil the lust of the flesh."

Galatians 5:22-25: "But the fruit of the Spirit is love, joy, peace, longsuffering, kindness, goodness, faithfulness, gentleness, self-control. Against such there is no law. And those who are Christ's have crucified the flesh with its passions and desires. If we live in the Spirit, let us also walk in the Spirit."

Based on these Scriptures, as we walk in the Spirit with the help of God's grace, we will bear spiritual fruit. This spiritual fruit is the evidence of the fact that we are God's children and have His divine nature in us. To say we are born again is not enough if there is no evidence of God's divine nature in our character. As we consciously walk daily with God in the spirit we will be step-by-step climbing the divine ladder of the fruit of the Spirit and we will continue to increase in the fruit of love, joy, peace, longsuffering, kindness, goodness, faithfulness, gentleness and self-control.

The Bible calls it the fruit of the Spirit, that is, it is just one fruit and not fruits and this fruit of the Spirit is revealed in us when we express the nine godly virtues.

What it means is that as God's children bearing His fruit, when we need to show love; love will be seen in us, when we need to be kind to others, kindness will be seen in us, and when we need for example to exercise self-control, this will be seen in us, we will not be out of control in our doings and responses.

Please refer to my book entitled *Self-control* for more on the importance of us exercising self-control.

There is a divine ladder of the fruit of the Spirit, and as we climb this ladder on a daily basis co-operating with the Holy Spirit, we will continue to grow in the expression of godly character and virtues. This will also help us to mature in our attitude and conduct towards God and man. Also, we will live a life for Christ, dead to ourselves and to our old ways. Our level of discernment towards what is godly will increase and we will be able to abstain more from ungodly and worldly ways.

14
Divine Ladder of Knowledge

The word 'knowledge' appears in the Bible 164 times, and the word 'know' (verb) appears 964 times. The word 'knowledge' means; to have information about a subject, thing or person. It is the state of knowing. It can also mean awareness, recognise, the sum of truths, facts and experiences accumulated over time. It can also mean discernment, perception, skill acquisition and to be acquainted with.

Here in specifics, I'm looking at climbing the divine ladder of knowledge towards the things of God, which will, of course, lead to other valuable forms of knowledge to mankind. Daniel 11:32b says:

> "But the people who know their God shall be strong and carry out great exploits".

The above Scripture indicates to us, that when we know God in spirit and in truth and act right with the knowledge of God, we will have strength and the doing of exploits for God will definitely follow. There is a general saying that 'knowledge is power.' John 8:32 says;

> "And you shall know the truth, and the truth shall make you free".

The truth of the word of God that makes us free is the truth that we have acted upon in God based on knowledge. As step-by-step we climb higher and higher on the divine ladder of the knowledge of God, we increase in strength and vigour in all things. Also, it helps to keep us from evil and sinning against the Almighty God because we will know what God expects from us and we will be able to do such by His grace. As we increase in the knowledge of Who God is, we are able to relate better with Him and please Him. Ephesians 3:19 says:

> "To know the love of Christ which passes knowledge; that you may be filled with all the fullness of God".

The word of God in the above Scripture makes it clear to us, that the knowledge of God's love, which is spiritual because love is a spiritual virtue, is higher than all other forms of godly knowledge such as; theological, intellectual, experience, etc. I must add that some people even know God as a miracle worker, which is true but all these other forms of knowledge of God are below the knowledge of God's love towards us because God is LOVE.

The knowledge of God's love towards us puts us in a place where we can also love God in return, love our fellow brothers and sisters and mankind in general. Knowing the love of Christ, which the Bible says 'passes knowledge' puts us in a place where we can be filled with all the fullness of God. The fullness of God which we have received by grace through Christ Jesus Our Lord and Saviour, includes The Holy Spirit of God, God's power, God's nature and attributes.

As we increase in the knowledge of God's love towards us, we are climbing step-by-step higher on the divine ladder of the knowledge of God and His fullness increases in us. This also puts us in a place where we can respond better to God's love, and we also can love God in return and ourselves and mankind as a whole. This then makes us complete in Christ Jesus.

15
Divine Ladder of Understanding
✂︎☙⚜☙✂︎

The word 'understanding' appears in the Bible 155 times and the word 'understand' appears 121 times. To 'understand' simply means; "to process, to attach a meaning, a reason, an interpretation to knowledge received" (Dictionary.com).

Understanding can be said to be how an individual has received or perceived information or knowledge given. It is making sense out of information, facts and acquired skills about a thing or subject, in order to accomplish a specific purpose or thing. Understanding, therefore, involves our minds because we have to think about the knowledge we have acquired for it to be meaningful to us. Understanding is the process of asking the questions like why, how and when on a subject matter.

I must also emphasise here, that after proper understanding of a subject, we move to the application, which is the act that leads to wisdom.

For instance a 'thing', we go from knowledge about a 'thing' to understanding the thing and, to wisdom of the thing.

And about a 'matter', we go from knowledge about the matter to understanding the matter to wisdom of the matter.

So, about God, we go from knowledge of godly issues to understanding godly issues to the wisdom of godly issues.

Therefore, in between knowledge and wisdom is UNDERSTANDING. Understanding is the process of digesting knowledge. We as God's children need to understand Our God and be able to see reason with Him so that we can be blessed by Him. 1 Chronicles 12:32 says:

> "Of the sons of Issachar who had understanding of the times, to know what Israel ought to do, their chiefs were two hundred; and all their brethren were at their command."

This is a very interesting verse of Scripture, which a lot of us know and recite, but the question is, have we taken the time to really ponder on it?

The fact that the sons of Issachar had understanding of the times means, that they were able to properly interpret the times, which is a gift from God. And from the proper interpretation of the times, they were able to take the right action and decision; hence all their brethren who didn't understand things had to depend on them for guidance, direction and leadership.

There is a divine ladder of understanding that we need to climb step-by-step by God's grace, so that we can properly understand God and the things around us. This way we can move on to applying wisdom.

Without understanding of a thing you cannot take the right action about that thing.

> "But there is a spirit in man, And the breath of the Almighty gives him understanding. Great men are not always wise, Nor do the aged always understand justice" (Job 32:8-9).

We can see that it is the LORD God Almighty that gives understanding to man. One of the easiest ways to know that a man has understanding of what he is saying is to watch his actions based on his words. Because, understanding will always lead to wisdom which is the application of what has been reasoned and thought through.

> "Give me understanding and I shall keep Your law; Indeed, I shall observe it with my whole heart" (Psalm 119:34).

We can see from this Scripture that the main reason why God's children keep disobeying Him is because they don't have an understanding of what God is saying. The question is that if there really and truly is understanding why would anyone deliberately want to offend the Almighty God?

A typical example is in the case of fire. We all know that fire is hot and that it can burn. Now if someone were to deliberately put his or her hand in fire, would you say that the person has acted based on an understanding of what fire can do? We will most probably not just regard such a person as not having understanding but, as a person that is out of his or her mind. Psalms 119:99 says:

> "I have more understanding than all my teachers, For your testimonies are my meditation".

This Scripture gives us the main secret to understanding God, which is *meditation.*

Meditation in a godly sense means; to ponder, think deep or reason deep. As we do this with God's word, our understanding of His word would increase.

> "A wise man will hear and increase learning, And a man of understanding will attain wise counsel" (Proverbs 1:5).

Here in this Scripture, we see the word of God giving us the complete process of understanding, which starts with acquiring knowledge through learning, then through learning moving on to attaching a meaning or reasoning through what we have learnt, and afterwards applying what we have learnt.

So it goes from Knowledge to Understanding and from understanding to Wisdom of a matter.

Understanding about God is acquired with the heart:

> "The heart of him who has understanding seeks knowledge, But the mouth of fools feeds on foolishness" (Proverbs 15:14).

The reason why the understanding heart still seeks knowledge is so that it can increase in understanding.

> "Consider what I say, and may the Lord give you understanding in all things" (2 Timothy 2:7).

We can see that the understanding that we need in order to be able to understand all things is from God and that there are different levels of understanding hence the divine ladder of understanding, which places people at different levels. I have made up my mind to step-by-step climb my God-given ladder of understanding on a daily basis in my life, how about you?

16
Divine Ladder of Wisdom
❌❦❧❌❧❦❌

This is another very important ladder we need to climb. The word wisdom appears in the Bible 227 times. I'm referring here to godly wisdom and not the wisdom of the world, which will pass away with the world. Wisdom is the practical application of knowledge that is understood in all endeavours of life and it includes; communication with people, the way we live our lives, conflict resolution, which is a big issue these days in the home, at work, at church and in the society at large.

Several relationships have been destroyed and a lot under strain because wisdom has been missing in the way issues have been handled. Proverbs 3:19 says:

> "The LORD by wisdom founded the earth; By understanding He established the heavens; By His knowledge the depths were broken up, And clouds drop down the dew."

We can see that the Almighty God Himself did all things in His wisdom, how much more you and I. We need to daily climb the divine ladder of God's wisdom step-by-step to be free from all unnecessary sorrow and troubles of life.

> "Then Moses called Bezalel and Aholiab and every gifted artisan in whose heart the LORD had put wisdom, everyone whose heart was stirred, to come and do the work" (Exodus 36:2).

Based on this Scripture, it is obvious that we definitely need God's wisdom to do the work of ministry, in a way that is pleasing to God. It is a very sad thing to be involved in ministry and for the Almighty God to be displeased with one's work. Climbing the divine ladder of God's wisdom will help us to do things right, always in the sight of God. I must say that even though we might be at different levels on this divine ladder of wisdom there is room to grow as we climb higher and higher.

"Now give me wisdom and knowledge, that I may go out and come in before this people; for who can judge this great people of Yours?" (2 Chronicles 1:10).

We see in the Bible how King Solomon became wise in decision making after God granted him his desire, following his request to God for wisdom as detailed in the above Scripture. We need the same wisdom from God too and we need to seek Him to increase us in His wisdom so that we can make decisions on a daily basis in alignment with His perfect divine will for our lives. Climbing the divine ladder of wisdom on a daily basis, helps to keep us away from trouble and sorrow, and keeps us heavenly focused, which I'm sure is the place we all want to be in for eternity.

"When wisdom enters your heart, And knowledge is pleasant to your soul, Discretion will preserve you; Understanding will keep you, To deliver you from the way of evil, From the man who speaks perverse things; from those who leave the path of uprightness To walk in the way of darkness" Proverbs 2:10-13).

17
Divine Ladder of Submission
❧❦❧❦❧❦

Dictionary.com defines the word submit as; "to give over or yield to the power or authority of another. To present for the approval, consideration or decision of another or others, for example, an application or a plan."

The word submit appears in the Bible 11 times and the word submission appears 4 times. The first person we need to submit to is the Almighty God. This we can do by living a life of willingly surrendering to His word and the Holy Spirit. James 4:7 says:

"Therefore submit to God. Resist the devil and he will flee from you."

Submission can be distinguished from obedience. Obedience is about obeying rules and commands handed down by authority, for example, a soldier in the army has to obey the command of a higher ranking officer whether he likes the word of command or not. If he doesn't he will have to face the consequences immediately. We can say that in the Old Testament, God worked with His people mainly based on this setting.

In submission, there is also authority and we respond to this authority willingly and voluntarily because there is also a relationship present, which we have to protect. In submission, there is love, respect and voluntary yielding to authority based on relationship, but in the case of obedience, a relationship with the person in authority doesn't have to be present. Although in our case we have a relationship with God and with our parents who we have to obey, you can obey authority and not be submissive to it.

Obedience is about your action mainly while submission is about your attitude mainly. This is why someone can grudgingly obey but you cannot grudgingly submit.

In submission, in order to understand fully what you are yielding to you can ask the question 'why' but in obedience you obey whether you understand the reason or not or whether you are allowed to ask questions or not.

Obedience can be enforced. This is why if the rules of a country are disobeyed you are punished, but you cannot enforce submission, which has to be done willingly, this is why a husband cannot force his wife to be submissive if she doesn't want to. Even Jesus, our Lord, did not force anyone to be His disciple and when some wanted to leave Him he let them go:

> "From that time many of His disciples went back and walked with Him no more. Then Jesus said to the twelve, "Do you also want to go?" But Simon Peter answered Him, 'Lord, to whom shall we go? You have the words of eternal life" (John 8:66-68).

Yes, we are to live a life of total obedience to God and His word. There is also a place in God through Jesus where we can develop a relationship with the Father, willingly submitting to the Holy Spirit of God; not just because God is going to smack us. This is why the Bible in (Ephesians 5:21-33), talks about us submitting to one another and that wives should submit to their own husbands and husbands should love their wives as Christ loved the church and gave Himself for her. So where there is love there is submission and where there is respect there is submission.

At the core of submission is relationship, whereas at the core of obedience are rules and commands that must be obeyed or you might have to face the immediate consequences of disobedience. I need to emphasize once more that we are both to obey God and submit to Him, and we are also told by God's word to obey and honour our parents. Both are important to us, but there is a difference in the two.

Whenever I say yes to God in submission, I'm automatically saying no to Satan and resisting him. When through submission I resist Satan, God backs me up and lifts me up.

Let us remind ourselves of the testimony of God regarding Job.

> "Then the LORD said to Satan, "Have you considered My servant Job, that there is none like him on earth, a blameless and upright man, one who fears God and shuns evil?" (Job 1:8).

The reason why the LORD had this testimony about Job was because he was living a life of submission to God.

There is a divine ladder of submission that as we climb it daily, we will have a testimony from God and men and God in return will bless and protect us as he did for Job. Job 1:10 says:

> "Have You not made a hedge around him, around his household, and around all that he has on every side? You have blessed the work of his hands, and his possessions have increased in the land."

This is the testimony of even the devil regarding Job. This is to let us know that God knows those who are His and protects them, and Satan too knows those who are God's and that they are protected by The Almighty and there is nothing he (the devil) can do about it.

God also wants us to be submissive to those who are in authority both in the church and in the government, as long as they are not leading us astray from God. God also expects His children to be submissive to one another:

> "Submitting to one another in the fear of God" (Ephesians 5:21).

> "Therefore submit yourselves to every ordinance of man for the Lord's sake, whether to the king as supreme, or to governors, as to those who are sent by him for the punishment of evildoers and for the praise of those who do good. For this is the will of God, that by doing good you may put to silence the ignorance of foolish men" (1 Peter 2:13-15).

> "Likewise you younger people, submit yourselves to your elders. Yes, all of you be submissive to one another, and be cloth with humility, for God resists the proud, But gives grace to the humble" (1 Peter 5:5).

In these Scriptures, we see submission coming out as a result of a relationship. My submission starts with the Almighty God and then extends to all the people my Bible tells me to submit to in the fear of God. As we climb this divine ladder of submission,

God's goodness will be ours in the name of Jesus. Another very important thing that will happen as we climb this divine ladder of submission is that God will make our enemies submit to us.

> "Happy are you, O Israel! Who is like you, a people saved by the LORD, The shield of your help And the sword of your majesty! Your enemies shall submit to you, And you shall tread down their high places" (Deuteronomy 33:29).

This was very true of Israel as long as they submitted to the Almighty God.

> "The haters of the Lord would pretend submission to Him, But their fate would endure forever. He would have fed them also with the finest of wheat; And with honey from the rock I would have satisfied you" (Psalm 81:15-16).

This Scripture is telling us that whoever is pretending that he or she is in submission to the Lord is a hater of God. So, our submission has to be genuine. Also, we can see that God wants to provide the best for those who are living a life of submission unto Him.

18
Divine Ladder of Forgiveness
❆❧❧❂❧❧❆

Forgiveness is another important divine ladder that we need to climb in order to maintain and build up relationships. The word 'forgive' simply means; to pardon, or to seize to feel resentful towards someone for what they have done wrong or appears to have done wrong. I personally don't think there is any human being on earth that will say someone has never wronged them at any time. We all at one point or another have offended someone or have been offended by others either knowingly or unknowingly. As God's children we have an example in our Lord and Saviour Jesus who came to pardon the sins of mankind, we also need to forgive our fellow human beings.

The word 'forgive' appears in the bible 53 times, 'forgiven' 43 times and 'forgiveness' 8 times. One thing is certain that a normal thinking human being will want God and man to forgive him or her when they are wrong, so we all ought to do the same too. Let's see what Jesus says in the Bible about forgiveness:

> "For if you forgive men their trespasses, your heavenly Father will also forgive you. But if you do not forgive men their trespasses, neither will your Father forgive your trespasses" (Matthew 6:14-15).

Climbing the divine ladder of forgiveness daily, helps us to acknowledge our wrong before God and man and asking for forgiveness from God also puts us in a place where we are able to forgive others also. I must admit, that it is easier to forgive when someone who has offended us accepts the fact that they are wrong, apologises and don't commit the offence again. However, life experiences have taught me that people don't always want to accept that they are wrong and it is not uncommon for people to refuse to apologise for the offence committed. This can in turn make forgiving somewhat difficult for us to do as human beings.

Having said this, my position from a godly perspective is that you should still forgive anyone who wrongs you even though you might have told them how you felt, and they have refused to accept their wrong doings while continuing to repeat the action and hurting your feelings every time. As a child of God, the onus is still on you to forgive, but in order to avoid a continuous recurrence of the hurtful situations, I would suggest you seek God for His wisdom and guidance, so that you can appropriately avoid putting yourself in a position where you might end up getting hurt, to the point of becoming so provoked and, reacting in a fleshy manner that is contrary to the will of God for your life.

One other thing I also want to highlight is that, whenever you forgive someone, which is something we are as Christians required to do all the time, you should try as much as possible to let them know in word or in deed that the matter is forgotten and that life goes on. I also want to add that un-forgiveness gives Satan an opportunity to take advantage of God's children. With regards to this, the Bible in (Matthew 9:2), says that:

> "Then behold, they brought to Him a paralytic lying on a bed. When Jesus saw their faith, He said to the paralytic, "Son, be of good cheer, your sins are forgiven you."

Jesus announced to the man before healing him that his sins were forgiven him. This serves as a kind of assurance and it helps build relationships.

> "Now whom you forgive anything, I also forgive. For if indeed I have forgotten anything, I have forgiven that one for your sakes in the presence of Christ, lest Satan should take advantage of us; for we are not ignorant of his devices" (2 Corinthians 2:10-11).

We see from this Scripture of 2 Corinthians, that Satan will move into the mind of someone practicing un-forgiveness to pollute and destroy it if care is not taken. There is absolutely nothing to gain if one is not forgiving, but everything to lose. So, when you forgive someone, you are actually helping yourself also and not just the offender. Lastly, I must also emphasise, that this divine ladder of forgiveness should not be seen as a license to live a sinful life, but is available for us in time of need. God has called us to live holy lives, and this will only happen if we cease from sinning and remain connected with His Holy Spirit.

19
Divine Ladder of Favour
✄⋐⟜⋒⟜⋐⟜⋒✄

The word 'favour' appears in the bible 96 times and it can be simply defined as; God's special affection towards us that releases His presence upon us and makes other people whether they are Christians or not want to help and co-operate with us. God has already granted me the grace to write a book on favour entitled *"God's Favour To You And Me"* in which I also listed all the scriptural verses in the Bible on the word favour for people to read, know and pray with for themselves. Please refer to the book for more on God's favour.

The important thing I would like to highlight in this book is that there is a divine ladder of favour that we have to believe God to climb daily step-by-step by His grace. As we climb up this ladder of favour, we will experience more and more of God's favour. The Bible clearly outlines various levels of favour, which I believe also represent various levels on the divine ladder of favour. Here are some examples of Bible verses, which outline the various levels of favour:

> "For You, O LORD, will bless the righteous; With favour You will surround him as with a shield" (Psalm 5:12).

> "And Hadad found great favour in the sight of Pharaoh, so that he gave him as wife the sister of his own wife, that is, the sister of Queen Tahpenes" (1 Kings 11:19).

> "For His anger is but for a moment, His favour is for life; Weeping may endure for a night, But joy comes in the morning" (Psalm 30:5).

> "And having come in, the angel said to her, "Rejoice highly favoured one, the Lord is with you; blessed are you among women" (Luke 1:28).

We can see from these four Scriptures that there are different levels of favour, which represents different levels on the divine ladder of favour.

The terms favour, great favour, highly favoured and favoured for life are definitely different levels of favour. It is my wish for you dear reader and myself that on a daily basis, we will continue to climb step-by-step, higher and higher on our divine ladder of favour in the name of Jesus. Amen!

20
Divine Ladder of Faith

The word 'faith' appears in the Bible 245 times. Faith in God simply means; to stand firm, to believe, to trust, to be firm, to endure and to be steadfast in God based on His word. Another simple definition of faith in God is, knowing God's word and acting on it. There is a divine ladder of faith that we need to climb daily step-by-step with the help of the Holy Spirit of God. As we climb daily, it becomes easier as time goes by for us to be able to trust in God at all times and this will definitely please the Almighty God who wants to be believed and trusted. Hebrews 11:6 says:

> "But without faith it is impossible to please Him, for he who comes to God must believe that He is, and that He is a rewarder of those who diligently seek Him".

Hebrews 11: 8 also says:

"By faith Abraham obeyed when he was called to go out to the place which he would receive as an inheritance. And he went out, not knowing where he was going."

This confirms the fact that faith in God leads us to obedience in God.

"For as the body without the spirit is dead, so faith without works is dead also" (James 2:26).

The evidence that we are step-by-step climbing the divine ladder of faith in God is reflected in our attitudes and actions towards the things of the kingdom of God, and also in the way we live our lives generally. For as many as are reading this book, I pray you will start to climb higher and higher the divine ladder of faith in the Almighty God in the name of Jesus. Amen!

21
Divine Ladder of Truth

Dictionary.com defines truth as; accuracy, as of position or adjustment, conformity with facts or reality. A verified or indisputable fact, the actual state of a matter, situation or thing.

The word 'truth' appears in the Bible 223 times and the word 'true' appears 80 times. A lot of the problems the world is facing today are because someone somewhere is not telling or accepting the truth with regard to a matter or thing. John 14:6 says:

> "Jesus said to him "I am the way, the truth, and the life. No one comes to the Father except through Me."

How wonderful the earth would be today if all men would embrace the—TRUTH which, is CHRIST JESUS? I also think that if everyone that claims to have given his or her life to Jesus happens to be relating and living by the truth, speaking the truth always and not telling lies, people who don't know Jesus, probably would have become more desirous of becoming part of the body of Christ. Speaking the truth on earth today is a very precious jewel, and it is quite difficult to come by. I'm calling on all my readers to make up their minds to step-by-step climb the divine ladder of truth because in doing so you will be a person of honour before the Almighty God and men. The truth is, it's only a matter of time before the truth and the lie are known:

> "Nevertheless I tell you the truth. It is to your advantage that I go away: for if I do not go away, the Helper will not come to you; but I depart, I will send Him to you" (John 16:7).

> "And I will pray the Father, and He will give you another Helper, that He may abide with you forever—the Spirit of

truth, whom the world cannot receive, because it neither sees Him nor knows Him; but you know Him, for He dwells with you and will be in you" (John 14:16-17).

"Therefore, putting away lying, Let each one of you speak truth with his neighbour, for we are members of one body" (Ephesians 4:25).

I've chosen the above three Scriptures to talk about speaking the truth. In the first Scripture we see our Lord and Saviour—who is The Truth itself, speaking the truth and we as His children need to be like Him, speaking and living in the truth.

The second Scripture is basically telling us, that if any one professing to be a disciple of Jesus Christ is into telling lies, he or she can be said not to have the Holy Spirit and doesn't belong to Jesus. We are told that the Holy Spirit is the Spirit of truth and that He dwells with us and in us as God's children, how then can it be possible to have a minister or a child of God that is always telling lies?

The third Scripture is encouraging us as God's children to speak the truth to one another as members of the same one body. So if as a Christian you are telling lies to a fellow Christian then you are telling lies to yourself.

It is of great importance for us to speak the truth at all times, live the truth and do everything in the character and nature of Christ who is—The Truth itself. This will make us a good example for the world to see and they will believe us when we speak or do things. Our step-by-step climb upward on the divine ladder of truth is proof that the ultimate TRUTH—which is Jesus Christ is in us and that we are His.

22
Divine Ladder of Character
❊〜✦❊〜✦❊

The character of a person is an account of values, behaviours, qualities, and peculiarities that makes up the individual. As God's children we are expected to have our character display godly traits which, are written in the Bible. There is a godly ladder of character which, we need to climb step-by-step on a daily basis, so that we can have the attitudes of our Lord and Master, Jesus Christ.

Throughout the Bible, we can see the royal character of God as it is revealed; it is entirely perfect. We are meant to have and express God's characters, grow daily, mature, develop and increase spiritually in regards to the manifestation of God's character from our inside to the outside. Here is a Scripture, which highlights the importance of us having a good character and pleasing God with our character:

"But also for this very reason, giving all diligence, add to your faith virtue, to virtue knowledge, to knowledge self-control, to self-control perseverance, to perseverance godliness, to godliness brotherly kindness, and to brotherly kindness love. For if these things are yours and abound, you will be neither barren nor unfruitful in the knowledge of our Lord Jesus Christ. For so an entrance will be supplied to you abundantly into the everlasting kingdom of our Lord and Saviour Jesus Christ." – 2 Peter 1:5-8:11

We can develop godly character by emulating Jesus, and before we do things asking ourselves questions like, what would Jesus do? Bearing the fruit of the spirit also helps us in building godly character.

23
Divine Ladder of Sacrifice
❊❦❧❊❦❧❊

The word 'sacrifice' as it is defined by Dictionary.com means: "The offering of an animal, plant or human life or of some material possession to a deity, as in propitiation or homage, the person, animal or thing so offered. The surrender or destruction of something prized or desirable for the sake of something considered as having a higher or more pressing claim."

The word 'sacrifice' appears 185 times in the Bible. I must say that God and Jesus have shown us examples of sacrificial giving as evidenced by the following Scriptures:

"For God so loved the world that He gave His only begotten Son, that whoever believes in Him should not perish but have everlasting life" (John 3:16).

Knowing the ministry of Jesus, God gave Jesus for us and He, Jesus, agreed to be given to us by His Father.

> "And being found in appearance as a man, He humbled Himself and became obedient to the point of death, even the death of the cross" (Philippians 2:8).

We also as God's children need to live a life of sacrifice unto the Lord; remember, like begets like. Step-by-step climbing the divine ladder of sacrifice enables us to give ourselves sacrificially back unto God. You might be wondering, how do I do this? My simple answer is that it is by living a life of dedication and commitment to the Lord. Giving God your time, resources, strength and showing concern and investing in His kingdom. I would also like to emphasise that evidence of our commitment to God's kingdom mandate, can also be seen by our showing concerns for people who are for instance in need, evangelising to the lost souls, and also helping those who are already in the kingdom to develop, mature and to get closer to God through our God-given talents and resources. Whatsoever we do sacrificially to others as God's children, is done directly for God.

From experience, I have come to recognise that it is almost impossible to show love to anyone without some form of sacrifice. I realise from my own experience, that at times when you sacrifice you deprive yourself of things, but guess what? God rewards.

> "I beseech you therefore, brethren, by the mercies of God, that you present your bodies a living sacrifice, holy,

acceptable to God, which is your reasonable service"
(Romans 12:1).

The best sacrifice I can give to God is that of my life, once
my life is given to God, to give anything else is easy. Once your
life is committed to a purpose, everything else about you follows
the purpose.

> "Therefore God also has highly exalted Him and
> given Him the name which is above every name, that
> at the name of Jesus every knee should bow, of those
> in heaven, and of those on earth, and of those under
> the earth, and that every tongue should confess that
> Jesus Christ is Lord, to the glory of God the Father"
> (Philippians 2:9-11).

The sacrifice that Jesus made for us as it is highlighted in
Scripture, led to His exaltation. The same will come to us as we
climb the divine ladder of sacrifice daily unto the Lord.

Some other ways by which we can sacrifice to God includes
service in His church, giving to the needy, giving people our time
to train them for the Lord's service and also for their personal
interest, etc.

We should do all our sacrificial giving and services unto the
Lord cheerfully and not grudgingly. Always keep in remembrance
how God blessed Abraham and his descendants for obeying
His word to sacrifice Isaac whom he loved unto Him (Genesis
22:1-18).

24
Divine Ladder of Tithing
❉❧❀❉❀❧❉

The word 'tithe' simply means one tenth (10%) of your incomes, of increases or profits from investments and businesses. The word 'tithe' appears in the Bible 17 times while 'tithes' appears 23 times, and has been recorded in the Bible as being practised even before God gave the commandments to Moses as we will see from the Bible.

I personally believe anyone who is in covenant relationship with God, should step-by-step climb this ladder by paying their tithes all the time and guess what, there are blessings that the Almighty God has promised to those who pay their tithes to Him.

Teaching on tithing is a whole book in itself but, God help me, I will in this book highlight the importance of climbing this divine ladder in obedience to God. Genesis 14:18-20 says:

> "Then Melchizedek king of Salem brought out bread and wine; he was the priest of God Most High. And he blessed him and said: "Blessed be Abram of God Most High, possessor of heaven and earth; And blessed be God Most High, Who has delivered your enemies into your hand." And he gave him a tithe of all."

Melchizedek who is a type of Jesus met Abram with bread and wine, which should immediately remind us of how Jesus

Christ also shared communion with his twelve disciples and also commanded us His Church, to also continue in the fellowship of communion with one another and with Him the Lord. Abram the Bible says, paid a tithe of all to Melchizedek whom the Bible refers to in Hebrews 7:1-3:

> "For this Melchizedek, king of Salem, priest of the Most High God, who met Abraham returning from the slaughter of the kings and blessed him, to whom also Abraham gave a tenth part of all, first being translated "king of righteousness," and then also king of Salem, meaning "king of peace," without father, without mother, without genealogy, having neither beginning of days nor end of life, but made like the Son of God remains a priest continually."

Abram paid his tithe out of an understanding of who God is and his relationship with God and not out of the law because we are not told anywhere in the Bible that God told Abram to pay. Paying to Melchizedek is likened to the same way we pay to our Lord and Saviour Jesus Christ today, so the principle has not changed at all.

> "But woe to you Pharisees! For you tithe mint and rue and all manner of herbs, and pass by justice and the love of God. These you ought to have done, without leaving the others undone" (Luke 11:42).

Here, we see Jesus talking about the paying of tithes and the other things that needed doing, He never said that it is not necessary for it to be paid in the dispensation of grace, but that we should also practice justice and love to be complete before God. Arguments have also risen as to whether you pay tithe from gross income or net. Net being after the government has taken their own taxes and gross being the full income without deductions. My position as I've previously explained in my book *Self-Control* is, that I think God should get His payments first before any government or man, so I pay my tithes as if I'm paying God first, which I do from gross and not net.

The reward for paying tithes is highlighted in Malachi 3:10-12:

> "Bring all the tithes into the storehouse, That there may be food in My house And try me now in this, "Says the Lord of Host, If I will not open for you the windows of heaven And pour out for you such blessing That there will not be room enough to receive it.
>
> And I will rebuke the devourer for your sakes, So that he will not destroy the fruit of your ground, Nor shall the vine fail to bear fruit for you in the field, Says the Lord of host; And all nations will call you blessed, For you will be a delightful land, Says the LORD of host."

God has promised to open the windows of heaven and to pour out such blessing that we will not have enough room to store them. He has promised to rebuke the devourer and that our finances and businesses will not fail and that all nations will call us blessed of the Lord. The blessing to be poured out is not just financial alone but all blessing from the Lord.

As we step-by-step climb this divine ladder of tithing in obedience, by paying our tithes always, God's blessing awaits us in the name of Jesus.

25
Divine Ladder of More and More of Jesus

This is a very wonderful God given ladder to climb because it keeps you thirsty for Jesus, to be like Him the more and to know Him the more. There are a few songs we sing in church about more and more of Jesus in our lives, and I pray it will be so.

"Let this mind be in you which was in Christ Jesus" (Philippians 2:5).

I believe having the mind of Christ will keep me hungry for more and more of Him. Jesus while on earth hungered for more and more of the Father in heaven, so He spent a good quality time in communion and prayer with the Father, we also need to do the same.

"So He Himself often withdrew into the wilderness and prayed" (Luke 5:16).

An interesting thing about this divine ladder of more and more of Jesus is in John 7:37-38:

> "On the last day, that great day of the feast, Jesus stood and cried out saying, "If anyone thirsts, let him come to Me and drink. He who believes in Me as the scripture has said, out of his heart will flow rivers of living water."

Here we see the link in between the thirst for more and more of Jesus and the overflowing of the Holy Spirit from our hearts. So one of the ways to keep the rivers of Living Water (The Holy Spirit) overflowing through us is to continue to thirst for more and more of Jesus by step-by-step climbing this divine ladder.

Apostle Paul in his letter to the church at Philippi says the following in Philippians 3:10-14:

> "That I may know Him and the power of His resurrection, and the fellowship of His sufferings being conformed to His death, if by any means, I may attain to the resurrection from the dead. Not that I have already attained, or am already perfected, but l press on, that l may lay hold of that for which Christ Jesus has also laid hold of me.

> Brethren, l do not count myself to have apprehended; but one thing l do, forgetting those things which are behind and reaching forward to those things which are ahead, I press toward the goal for the prize of the upward call of God in Christ Jesus."

We can see here the thirst for more and more of Jesus by Apostle Paul, letting us know that in the Lord Jesus there is nothing like knowing it all, already arrived or having enough of the Master on the inside. We have to keep the hunger and thirst in the same way we have to keep breathing air and eating physical food to keep alive on earth. There is great reward for this, which is that we shall be filled with the Holy Spirit of God to the overflow so that people around us can also benefit from us.

> "And we know that the Son of God has come and has given us an understanding that we may know Him who is true; and we are in Him who is true, in His son Jesus Christ. This is the true God and eternal Life" (1 John 5:20).

This knowing and being in Jesus is a continuous state and not a one off state. Climbing this divine ladder of more and more of Jesus also ensures that the eternal life of God keeps flowing into us, and so shall it be in the name of Jesus.

3

Step-by-Step Divine Ladders from Twenty-Six to Fifty-Two

ርቋ৪৩ርቋ৪৩

26
Divine Ladder of Service Unto the Lord

The word 'service' is often used not just in church but also in the circular world. The word 'service' taken from the Collins English dictionary simply means an act of help or assistance, the state of availability or use which can be by the public.

I want to narrow this definition to mean the state of availability for use by the Almighty God. That is making one's self available for use by God.

The word to 'serve' appears in the Bible 214 times and 'service' appears 105 times. There is a divine ladder of serving the Lord that God's children need to climb daily. There are different forms of services that we can render unto the Lord; I will want to say that one of the best types is the one that is rendered willingly out of a cheerful heart. The Bible is also filled with promises of reward for serving the Lord, even though this should not be the primary reason for service, but it is worth mentioning because God has mentioned them in His word because He knows man better than man knows himself.

I personally render my service unto the Lord willingly and cheerfully out of my love for God and regard for the relationship I have with the Lord.

I need to mention that understanding this divine ladder also spills over to the way we relate to other people we are meant to serve, say for example at your place of work. Even though you are getting paid for what you do, you still need to do it cheerfully and honestly with all dedication as unto the Lord. We are told to do so by the Bible, because as we show full dedication to our employers and clients, the Almighty God gets the glory when they get to know that we are His children.

I also would like to add that it is impossible to serve God diligently if you cannot serve the man you can see diligently:

> "Bondservants, be obedient to those who are your masters according to the flesh, with fear and trembling, in sincerity of heart, as to Christ; not with eye service, as men-pleasers, but as bondservants of Christ, doing the will of God from the heart, with goodwill doing service, as to the Lord and not to men, knowing that whatever good anyone does, he will receive the same from the Lord, whether he is a slave or free." – Ephesians 6:5-8

As we can see from the above Bible verses, service is related to the heart and also the fact that even though you might be working for your employer you need to render your services as unto the Lord with all sincerity of heart and goodwill because in your doing so, God is glorified. We are also told that from the Lord you will receive a reward; I believe this reward is not just talking about the wages you will be getting from your employer.

> "So you shall serve the LORD your God, and He will bless your bread and your water. And I will take sickness away from the midst of you. No one shall suffer miscarriage or be barren in your land; I will fulfil the number of your days" (Exodus 23:25-26).

Here again we see God in His word promising to reward your service and mine unto Him all the days of our lives on the earth as long as we continue to climb this divine ladder of serving the Lord without looking back.

In case you are desiring to serve the Lord but, feel that you are not in a position to because you have not been given any role in the church, my advice is that you should speak to the church leadership and ask them how you can help. You can make yourself available or you can suggest to leadership what you think needs to be done and let them know that you are available to do it. I'm very sure by the time you say this to them, they will certainly find something for you to do. You can also join a group in the church like the evangelism or prayer group, which I'm sure can always do with some more people.

Once more as you step-by-step climb this divine ladder of service unto the Lord, goodness awaits you from Him. Amen.

27
Divine Ladder of Trust in the Lord
ЖᏋᎤᏉᏒᎤᏉ

The word 'trust' simply means to rely upon someone or a thing. In the context of my writing I would want to see trust to mean reliance upon God based on His integrity, power, strength and His Word.

The word 'trust' appears in the Bible 125 times and in words and in deeds God is to be trusted. There is a divine ladder of trust in the Lord that God's children need to climb daily so that we can get better results in our lives from Him. God wants to be trusted by His children and it is His strong desire that He be trusted so that He can do the things He has said in His word that He will do.

We need to understand that Satan is doing everything possible to make God's children distrust God because He knows that if this happens God is never going to be pleased with such an individual. Even you and I as human beings feel uncomfortable around people who distrust us especially if there are no foundations for distrust.

> "Trust in the LORD with all your heart, And lean not on your own understanding; In all your ways acknowledge Him, and He shall direct your paths" (Proverbs 3:5-6).

The above Scripture and several other Scriptures in the Bible encourages us to trust in the Lord with all our heart. This means that we are to put all our eggs in the basket of the Lord and not just some. At all times, I depend on the Lord for direction and guidance in all my doings. My trust is completely in Him and nothing more or less.

> "For in Him we live and move and have our being" (Acts 17:28a).

If this Scripture is true for you as I know it is true for me, then we need to daily climb this divine ladder.

> "The Lord is my strength and my shield; My heart trusted in Him, and I am helped; Therefore my heart greatly rejoices, And with my song I will praise Him" (Psalm 28:7).

We can see from this Scripture above that the heart of man is the centre of trust in the Lord. I want to see the heart of man here to mean his spirit and soul. As I've explained in one of my books about the mind, the mind of a man is in his soul, it is an immaterial part of man. So trust in the Lord is not with the brain of man but his spirit and soul and once your spirit and soul is in anything then your body will follow.

To confirm what I've said with the Scripture above, it goes on to say therefore my heart rejoices greatly. To rejoice is to recycle your joy and we know that joy is spiritual and part of the fruit of the spirit.

As we start to trust in the Lord with all our heart and step-by-step climb the divine trust ladder, may we be filled with rejoicing and may we be filled with praises unto our God in the name of Jesus. Amen.

28
Divine Ladder of the Overflow of the Holy Spirit
❊❧❦❊❧❦❊

The word 'overflow' simply means; to run over, to have the content of something in a container overfull to spilling over. An example can be to pour water in a glass till it is filled and to keep pouring, you get an overflow. I'm looking at the overflow of the Holy Spirit of God and not just at having the Holy Spirit, in the same way, you can have some water in a glass, but not to the measure of overflowing.

I believe there is a divine ladder of the overflow of the Holy Spirit that we can step-by-step climb daily because God wants to pour out His Spirit upon His children without measure so that people who don't know God can come and drink of Him too by getting to know Him (God).

> "On the last day, that great day of the feast, Jesus stood and cried out saying, "If anyone thirst, let him come to Me and drink. He who believes in Me, as the scriptures has said, out of his heart will flow rivers of living water" (John 7:37-38).

As we climb this divine ladder because we thirst for more and more of the Holy Spirit and believe in Jesus, the flowing of rivers of Living Water through us, become sources and channels of spiritual blessings for those around us and for our nations in the name of Jesus. This will also draw people to accept Jesus through this wonderful God given experience. It is an overflow without limitation of the Holy Spirit.

This divine ladder enables us to experience the overflowing fullness of God's Spirit in our lives.

29
Divine Ladder of First Fruits

Some might be surprised that I see the release of first fruits unto the Lord, as a divine ladder we need to climb step-by-step as God's children. The principle of releasing our first fruits unto God is a confirmation that we love God and that we are willing to put Him first in all things.

I will briefly mention the types of first fruits which, in RCCG are now being taught so that we can practice them and be blessed for our love for Him.

1. **The first fruits of increase of wages:** (Proverbs 3:9-10) says, "Honour the Lord with your possessions, And with the first fruits of all your increase; So your barns will be filled with plenty and your vats will overflow with new wine."

This is the first fruits of increase say of wages, salaries or an increase in the already established profits of a business. An example is in the case of an individual, who gets a pay rise from work and last month's wages were £1500 and this month is £1600, the increase of £100 is the first fruit which is paid as a one off for that increment.

2. **The First fruit sacrifice:** This is when we give as a sacrifice unto the Lord a whole month's salary, all the business profits, a whole day's or week's wages unto the Lord or when we commit say a working day of our lives to the Lord's service sacrificially.

    1 John 3:16: "By this we know love, because He laid down His life for us. And we also ought to lay down our lives for the brethren."

    The same happened in (Genesis Chapter 22), when Abraham offered up Isaac unto the Lord.

3. **Redemption of the firstborn:** (Exodus13:12-13), "That you shall set apart to the LORD all that open the womb, that is every first born that comes from an animal which you have; the male shall be the LORD's But every firstborn of a donkey you shall redeem with a lamb; and if you will not redeem it then you shall break its neck. And all the firstborn of man among your sons you shall redeem."
This is done in our times by bringing a price offering unto the Lord for your first male child and even in the case where a

family does not have a male child a redemption price offering can be brought for the daughter, since she is also your first seed.

As we do these, we are step-by-step climbing the divine ladder of first fruit offerings and we will be greatly blessed by God.

Remember how Abraham and Hannah were blessed because they offered their first fruits unto the Lord and their blessings were irreversible.

> "And the LORD visited Hannah, so that she conceived and bore three sons and two daughters. Meanwhile the child Samuel grew before the LORD" (1 Samuel 2:21).

Hannah experienced this because she gave her first son Samuel fully into the service of the Lord. I leave you as my reader in the hands of the Holy Spirit to direct you as to how you should step-by-step climb this divine ladder of first fruits, which to the glory of God I have already started climbing.

30
Divine Ladder of Comfort
❇❧☙❇❧☙❇

The word 'comfort' simply means; to soothe, console, reassure, to relieve, to ease either from pain, emotional distress, or any form of unrest which can also be spiritual.

The word 'comfort' appears in the Bible 59 times and as we climb the divine ladder of comfort, not only are we comforted by the Lord, but we will be able to comfort people around us who need it. As the saying goes you can't give what you don't have.

"Even when I walk through the dark valley of death, I will not be afraid, for You are close beside me. Your rod and Your staff, they protect and comfort me" (Psalm 23:4). NLT

This popular verse of Scripture is letting us know that our Lord, the great Shepherd, is always with us and watching over us, even when we are passing through dangerous moments of our lives and we are not sure of what is going to happen to us. The same way a shepherd protects his sheep with his rod, to guide them away from danger and dangerous attackers we also experience the same from the Lord.

Climbing the divine ladder of comfort, gives us the assurance that whenever we need comfort it will be provided by the Lord:

"For the Lord will comfort Zion, He will comfort all her waste places; He will make her wilderness like Eden, And her desert like the garden of the Lord; Joy and gladness will be found in it, Thanksgiving and the voice of melody" (Isaiah 51:3).

"Now we exhort you, brethren, warn those who are unruly, comfort the faint-hearted, uphold the weak, be patient with all" (1 Thessalonians 5:14).

You have to be climbing the divine ladder of comfort to be in a place to comfort others:

> "Now may Our Lord Jesus Christ Himself, and Our God and Father, who has loved us and given us everlasting consolation and good hope by grace, Comfort your hearts and establish you in every good word and work" (2 Thessalonians 2:16-17).

31
Divine Ladder of Anointing

The word anointing is quite a common word we use in the Church. The word 'anointing' appears in the Bible 27 times and the word 'anoint' appears 35 times. To anoint simply means, to 'rub upon', to consecrate. In most cases, as we will see in the Bible, oil was used, which indicates the Holy Spirit of the Living God. The person anointed is now separated for God's service and has been chosen by God for this.

With the anointing, comes responsibility for service as authorised by God Himself. The anointing can be said to be the burden removing, yoke destroying power of God. It can also be said to be God's supernatural ability and power, coming upon an individual to empower them to do things they couldn't do before.

"It shall come to pass in that day That his burden will be taken away from your shoulder, And the yoke from your neck, And the yoke will be destroyed because of the anointing oil" (Isaiah 10:27).

There is a divine ladder of anointing that we can step-by-step climb on a daily basis to receive fresh anointing to do the work of the kingdom of God on earth. This will empower us to be able to do things which the natural man cannot do for the Almighty God.

"How God anointed Jesus of Nazareth with the Holy Spirit and with power, who went about doing good and healing all who were oppressed by the devil, for God was with Him" (Acts 10:38).

We can see that even Jesus in His ministry needed the anointing of the Holy Spirit, to do good and to heal and deliver people from sicknesses and diseases and from all satanic oppressions and possessions, how much more you and I. We need the anointing on a daily basis to be able to do the work of ministry like Jesus did.

Anointing also helps us to constantly maintain our victory over the devil and his cohorts and to be effective in our ministry of God's kingdom. So I'm not talking about the anointing of yesterday which might have ended with yesterday but a fresh oil on a daily basis which we can receive by God's grace:

"But my horn You have exalted like a wild ox; I have been anointed with fresh oil" (Psalm 92:10).

We can increase in anointing with the outpouring of daily fresh oil from God, with the step-by-step climbing of the divine ladder of anointing, which has to be continuous so that we can move from one level of anointing to another.

This is necessary because without the continuous anointing of the Holy Spirit, the work of ministry will be difficult since it is spiritual and not physical. The anointing of the Holy Spirit enables us to carry out our own given specific assignments by God, so that people can be anointed to carry out different functions for the kingdom of God and hence have certain gifts, which others might not have. An example of this is the gift of prophecy, or word of knowledge or working of miracles.

"But you have an anointing from the Holy One, and you know all things" (1 John 2:20).

"But the anointing which you have received from Him abides in you, and you do not need that anyone teach you; but as the same anointing teaches you concerning all things and is true, and is not a lie, and just as it has taught you, you will abide in Him" (1 John 2:27).

Climbing this divine ladder also helps us to abide in the anointing of the Holy Spirit of God. Amen!

32
Divine Ladder of Power
ℵ☙❧⊙❧☙ℵ

The word 'power' is a word almost everyone is familiar with. It appears in the Bible 245 times. Power simply means; ability, capacity, vigour, means, substance, force and wealth required to act or to get something done. The source of power can be spiritual, mental, physical, political, financial, industrial, military and influential and so on. The most powerful source of power is spiritual. Once an individual has gotten spiritual power from God, other forms of power are usually present.

There is a divine ladder of power ordained by the Almighty God that He wants His children to climb step-by-step, with the help of the Holy Spirit. Power from God enables us to do things.

We know that the Almighty God is Omnipotent, meaning He has all powers and that He has delegated powers also to us His children:

> "But as many as received Him, to them gave He power to become the sons of God, even to them that believe on His name" (John 1:12) KJV.

There is power in being a child of God and growing in Him because this enables us to be like our Father in heaven. As we grow from being a child of God to sons and daughters of God we increase in God's power and ability.

"But you shall receive power when the Holy Spirit has come upon you; and you shall be witnesses to Me in Jerusalem, and in all Judea and Samaria, and to the end of the earth" (Acts 1:8).

Here we see the Holy Spirit of God as the source of power to do what needs to be done with boldness. Baptism of the Holy Spirit releases God's power to us and enables us to keep climbing step-by-step up the divine ladder of power, higher and higher and doing what God expects from us His children on a daily basis. From the Scripture above, we can see that the power of the Holy Spirit is for all God's children, to witness and win souls into His kingdom, it is not for specific people but for all.

33
Divine Ladder of Seeking God's Face
✂❧⤜✂❧⤜✂

The word 'seek' simply means; "to search for, to enquire about something, to try finding something by searching or questioning." Dictionary.com.

The word 'seek' appears in the Bible 243 times, 'seeking' appears 38 times and 'sought' appears 111 times.

There is a divine ladder of seeking the face of the Lord that we step-by-step need to climb daily so that we can discover something new about God, have a personal experience of Him and understand Him better. This seeking has to be continuous because there is no end to seeking God's face.

> "And you will seek Me and find Me, when you search for Me with all your heart" (Jeremiah 29:13).

I pray that you will find God as you search for Him with all your heart in the name of Jesus. By heart, I mean the heart which represents your spirit and soul.

> "But seek first the kingdom of God and His righteousness and all these things shall be added to you" (Matthew 6:33).

> "But without faith it is impossible to please Him, for he who comes to God must believe that He is, and that He is a rewarder of those who diligently seek Him." – Hebrews 11:6

From the two Scriptures above we can see that there are rewards in seeking after God and this seeking also includes searching the word of God for questions that we might have within our souls about Him.

34
Divine Ladder of Diligence
❈❦❧❈❦❧❈

The word diligence simply means, putting in the constant and persistent effort required in order to accomplish a goal or a task.

I personally believe that we need to be diligent to make it to heaven and also to succeed in whatever we do. The word diligence appears in the Bible 9 times and diligent 17 times.

There is a divine ladder of diligence that we need to step-by-step climb daily to fulfil our goals and destiny in the Lord Jesus. We could say this is no easy task, but remember what Jesus said in (2 Corinthians 12:9a):

> "And He said to me, "My grace is sufficient for you, for My strength is made perfect in weakness."

There is grace, which God Has made available to us, so that we can do the things we really have made up our minds to do.

> "Be diligent to present yourself approved to God, a worker who does not need to be ashamed, rightly dividing the word of truth" (2 Timothy 2:15).

Diligence as we are told here will make us present ourselves approved before God. And if we are approved before God then nobody can disapprove of us. Diligence helps us to understand what God expects from us and how to act accordingly with understanding.

Diligence will also help us in our employment, businesses and studies, which will help us reflect God's glory in all that we do. Diligence is required when we talk about living holy, righteous and being prayerful:

"The lazy man does not roast what he took in hunting, But diligence is man's precious possession" (Proverbs 12:27).

As we step-by-step climb the ladder of diligence, may precious possessions be ours in the name of Jesus. Amen.

Quotes on Diligence

1. "What we hope to do with ease, we must learn first to do with diligence." – *Samuel Johnson.*
2. "Patience and Diligence, like faith Remove Mountains." – *William Penn.*
3. "Building our homes as fortresses of righteousness for protection from the world takes constant labour and diligence" – *Joseph B. Wirthlin.*

35
Divine Ladder of Direction

If there is one thing we all need on a daily basis it will be Godly direction. We all need the Lord to direct our paths on earth as we journey through earth to heaven. There is a divine ladder of direction that we all need to climb daily step-by-step to be on the right path to heaven and to fulfil our purposes and goals on earth. The word 'direct' appears in the Bible 12 times and 'direction' appears 11 times.

The Bible is full of examples of the Almighty God giving direction to His people in order to get them to their expected end. The word direct simply means; to guide to a place, to a successful accomplishment, to a destination, to orientate towards a goal or a purpose, to motivate towards good steps, give useful advice, information or instructions. To lead. Dictionary.com

"In all your ways acknowledge Him, And He shall direct your paths" (Proverbs 3:6).

"Direct my steps by Your word, And let no iniquity have dominion over me." (Psalm 119:133).

"And the Lord went before them by day in a pillar of cloud to lead the way, and by night in a pillar of fire to give them light, so as to go by day and night. He did not take away the pillar of cloud by day or the pillar of fire by night from before the people" (Exodus 13:21-22).

It is very interesting to know that the Lord we serve wants to give us round the clock direction so that both day and night we do not miss our directions in life, as we journey to heaven. Remember the children of Israel journeyed to the promise land and got there.

We also will arrive at our final destination—heaven, safe and sound in the name of Jesus. Amen.

36
Divine Ladder of Zeal
✕⌘✕⌘✕

The word 'zeal' simply means; fervent enthusiasm (passion) about a cause, position or interest. It is a fervent (burning) adherence to a position or a cause which is in most cases, almost impossible to change. It is an immovable position or stand about a cause or ideology which in most cases can be a belief or religion.

The word 'zeal' appears in the Bible 22 times. It is very different from desire in the sense that a desire which can be a wish, request or a want might depend on somebody else to fulfil but zeal is dependent mainly on you the individual. Whatever the other person thinks or feels about it, is of no concern to you. Let me give an example with two Scriptures:

> "I know all the things that you do, that you are neither hot nor cold. I wish you were one or the other!" (Revelations 3:15) NLT.

This is the wish (desire) of Jesus concerning the lukewarm church in the book of revelation. So at times our desires depend on other people to establish but zeal doesn't. Your zeal about a cause or position depends mainly on you and you are ready with God's understanding and wisdom to do everything possible to keep your zeal alive.

Let's look at Jesus now in the place of Zeal.

"Now the Passover of the Jews was at hand, and Jesus went up to Jerusalem. And He found in the temple those who sold oxen and sheep and doves, and the money changers doing business.

When He had made a whip of cords, He drove them all out of the temple, with the sheep and the oxen, and poured out the changers' money and overturned the tables. And He said to those who sold doves,

"Take these things away! Do not make My Father's house a house of merchandise! "Then His disciples remembered that it was written, 'Zeal for Your house has eaten Me up." – John 2:13-17

Here we see Jesus taking a firm stand not bothering about what the money changers and everybody else taught or felt. He knew that his position would offend the Pharisees who directly or indirectly had allowed trading in the temple for financial gains but He ignored all that. His zealous position was expressed irrespective of what everybody else taught or felt.

I would like to make it clear that the step-by-step climbing of the divine ladder of zeal for the Lord, doesn't mean that we have to hurt or kill anyone to show that we have a zeal for the Lord. This is not godly, Jesus did not have to hurt or kill anyone to express His zeal and in fact He drove them out of the temple because the temple was His Father's house and not theirs.

With zeal your position is immovable, no matter what the opposition says or does, it is the zeal of the Lord.

There is a divine ladder of zeal that we need to step-by-step climb in Christ Jesus, which keeps us on cause and position always for the Lord come what may. As we do this, the Lord Himself will continue to make sure that the zeal of His house and kingdom will continue to eat us up, which means that our lives are on the altar of God and is no more ours.

The zeal of the Lord upon us puts us in a place where we are ready to do things for the Lord irrespective of what anybody thinks or does to us. The early church was able to face persecution for the Lord because God's zeal had eaten them up. I personally believe that the zeal of God upon Jesus was the reason why He was able to go to the cross for us and we also need to have the same zeal for the things of God.

> "So the Angel who spoke with me said to me, "Proclaim, saying, 'Thus says the LORD of host: "I am zealous for Jerusalem And for Zion with great zeal" (Zechariah 1:14).

Zion here is talking about God's people which today is the church of Jesus. So if God is zealous for us, we also need to be zealous for Him.

37
Divine Ladder of the Presence of the Lord
❊☙✦❂✦☙❊

The word 'presence' talks about the state of being present with someone, with people or being at a place. It can also mean to be nearby or in close proximity to a person or place. It appears in the Bible 156 times. The presence of the Almighty God is what every child of God should strongly desire; the same way children want to be close to their parents. There is a divine ladder of God's presence that we can step-by-step climb as God's children, on a daily basis, which will continue to draw us closer and closer to God.

The closer we are to Him, the more of Him we know and the more of Him is in us. The more God rubs on us the more of Him we manifest.

> "You will show me the path of life; In Your presence is fullness of joy; At Your right hand are pleasures forevermore" (Psalm 16:11).

In the presence of the Almighty God, we are filled with both joy and pleasures forevermore.

> "For You have made him most blessed forever; You have made him exceedingly glad with Your presence" (Psalm 21:6).

The presence of the Lord is blessing and gladness forevermore. It also keeps us from stumbling and makes us faultless before God.

> "Now to Him who is able to keep you from stumbling, And to present you faultless Before the presence of His

glory with exceeding joy, To God our Saviour, who alone is wise, Be glory and majesty, Dominion and power, Both now and forever. Amen" (Jude 24:25).

38
Divine Ladder of Correction

This divine ladder would probably be one a lot of us don't particularly like. My own life experiences have shown me that the average human being at times finds it difficult to accept correction. I have had to, with the help of God train myself to accept correction when I'm wrong and this is irrespective of the person God is using to correct me. To 'correct' as defined by dictionary.com means; "to set or make true, accurate or right; remove errors or faults from. To scold, rebuke, or punish in order to improve."

The word 'correction' appears in the Bible 18 times while the word 'correct' appears 9 times. There is a divine ladder of correction that God's children need to climb daily step-by-step, so that they can grow in the Lord and be right before Him. God corrects His children mainly through His word, our earthly parents and those who are in charge of us in our places of learning which includes the church environment.

> "Harsh discipline is for him who forsakes the way, And he who hates correction will die" (Proverbs 15:10).

"All scripture is given by inspiration of God, and is profitable for doctrine, for reproof, for correction, for instruction in righteousness, that the man of God may be complete, thoroughly equipped for every good work" (2 Timothy 3:16-17).

The second Scripture is telling us that without teaching, correction and instruction in righteousness it is not possible to properly equip us for every good work in the Lord.

A lot of times when we talk about correction, the minds of a lot of adults go straight to children, creating an impression that adults are always right and children always wrong. If we want to be honest with ourselves, there are a lot of adults who behave like children and are refusing correction because they see themselves as above correction. I want to say that no one is above correction from God's perspective, and we must all see it so.

The Gospel we preach for example is aimed at helping people correct their lives before the Almighty God, but does this happen all the time?

"A fool despises his father's instruction, But he who receives correction is prudent" (Proverbs 15:5).

"Correct your son, and he will give you rest; Yes, he will give delight to your soul" (Proverbs 29:17).

As we put ourselves in a place where we allow God to correct us through the means He sees best at any point in time of our lives, we will be step-by-step climbing this divine ladder of correction and the Lord will delight in us and He will see us as His own children. May it be so in the name of Jesus. Amen.

39
Divine Ladder of Salvation
(Staying Saved in the Lord)
❊❦❧❊❊❦❧❊

This divine ladder of salvation (staying saved in the Lord) is the divine ladder that all who have given their lives to Jesus have started with, and we need to continue in it and not stay stagnant or come down from it.

I want to look at salvation to mean; the act of being saved (which has been accomplished by Our Lord and Saviour Jesus Christ), and staying saved, which we have to do with the help of the Lord.

> "Therefore my beloved, as you have always obeyed, not as in my presence only, but now much more in my absence, work out your own salvation with fear and trembling" (Philippians 2:12).

Apostle Paul is not talking about our initial salvation at the cross of Calvary, which has been forever settled, but he is saying to us to remain saved by progressing in our Christian lives and building godly character, which requires us to be consciously co-operating with the Holy Spirit in us.

Part of staying saved will also happen, when we continue working on our relationship with the Lord daily, with the help of His grace and fellowshipping with one another so that we can continue to sharpen each other in the journey of salvation (staying saved).

> "So Christ was offered once to bear the sins of many. To those who eagerly wait for Him He will appear a second time, apart from sin, for salvation" (Hebrews 9:28).

This Scripture is talking about the consummation of our salvation, which will happen at the time of the rapture when Our Lord Jesus will come back to take home those who have remained saved in Him.

> "And do this, knowing the time, that now it is high time to awake out of sleep; for now our salvation is nearer than when we first believed" (Romans 13:11).

Here also we are encouraged to remain faithful in the Lord, for the end road of our salvation is nearer than when we first started the journey of salvation, by giving our lives to Jesus.

> "But he who endures to the end shall be saved" (Matthew 24:13).

As we keep enduring the Christian race and step-by-step climb the divine ladder of salvation daily, we will remain saved to the end in the name of Jesus. Amen.

40
Divine Ladder of Exploits
✄ᤠᤠᤠᤠᤠ✄

The word 'exploit' as explained by Dictionary.com means; "a striking or notable deed especially one that is spirited, noble or heroic. To promote, to advance, to utilise an occasion or opportunity to its fullest potential.

The word 'exploits' appears in the Bible just once, but it is still very important to mention it as a God-given ladder that we need to climb step-by-step and to keep doing exploits for God and His kingdom.

> "But the people who know their God shall be strong, and carry out great exploits" (Daniel 11:32b).

Hear we see the link between knowing God, which leads to being strong, which then leads to doing exploits for our God. Reason being that to do the extraordinary requires divine knowledge and strength from the Almighty God. I pray that as you read this book you will start to climb the divine ladder of exploits, to do what nobody has done yet for God in the name of Jesus.

I believe that as we start to do exploits for God's kingdom, God will also empower us to do exploits in our own lives also in the name of Jesus.

I need to mention that there is still a lot that needs to be done for God's kingdom, there are still billions of souls unsaved, we still have the hungry and the destitute all over the world that need help and there are still a lot of areas in the world that need peace, which you and I can be used by the Almighty God to help present through the resolving of conflicts as the Lord will permit.

41
Divine Ladder of Endurance
❧❦✠❦❧

The word 'endurance' simply means; to be able to bear pain, hardships, trials and adverse situations. It appears in the Bible just twice while the word 'endure' appears 42 times. There is a divine ladder of endurance that God's children need to climb on a daily basis, so that we don't give up on our calling in the Almighty God, and so that at the end we can receive a reward. I must emphasise that the grace to endure has already been released unto us by the Almighty God. We also need to remember that Jesus also endured in His ministry on earth and He was able to fulfil His goals as a man, we can do the same too in the name of Jesus.

As we climb this divine ladder of endurance daily we are able to keep enduring until the end.

"For you have need of endurance, so that after you have done the will of God, you may receive the promise" (Hebrews 10:36).

Whenever we try to obey God there is always a resistance either from within or without, but we have to endure and overcome this resistance in order to please God.

"Therefore we also, since we are surrounded by so great a cloud of witnesses, let us lay aside every weight, and the sin which so easily ensnares us, and let us run with endurance the race that is set before us, looking unto Jesus, the author and finisher of our faith, who for the joy that was set before Him endured the cross, despising the shame, and has sat down at the right hand of the throne of God." – Hebrews 12:1-2

We know very well the end result of the endurance of our Lord and Saviour Jesus Christ, the exaltation that God bestowed upon Him, the same will be ours if we endure to the end.

"Indeed we count them blessed who endure. You have heard of the perseverance of Job and seen the end intended by the Lord that the Lord is very compassionate and merciful" (James 5:11).

"And we labour working with our own hands. Being reviled, we bless; being persecuted, we endure" (1 Corinthians 4:12).

"You therefore must endure hardship as a good soldier of Jesus Christ" (2 Timothy 2:3).

We are called by God to a ministry of endurance because as we do the will of our Master we should expect opposition from those who are against us and we need to endure and not give up. As we do this daily, God releases unto us the grace and wisdom required so as to be able to endure to the end. At the end of our endurance journey is a reward from the Lord.

"And you will be hated by all for My name's sake. But he who endures to the end shall be saved" (Mark 13:13).

This is a word of encouragement from our Lord and Saviour Jesus Christ.

Quote: Every calamity is to be overcome by endurance – *Virgil*.

42
Divine Ladder of Inheritance
❊❦❧❊❧❦❊

The word 'inheritance' simply means; birthright, portion, possessions (both spiritual and physical) that one has the right to have as a result of position or birth. We are God's children by adoption, therefore, have rights to possess what God has given to us; both physical and spiritual inheritances.

As we step-by-step climb this divine ladder of inheritance, we begin to possess all that is our portion both physical and spiritual to the glory of the Lord.

The word 'inheritance' appears in the Bible 246 times and can I say that one of the best things that can ever happen to us as God's children, is for the Almighty God to see us and choose us as His own inheritance. When God chooses us as His own inheritance this means that we fully belong to Him, the very source of all good blessings spiritual, material and physical. And whoever belongs to God is one with Him the very source of life.

> "Blessed is the nation whose God is the LORD, The people He has chosen as His own inheritance" (Psalm 33:12).

> "Be strong and of good courage, for to this people you shall divide as an inheritance the land which 1 swore to their fathers to give them" (Joshua 1:6).

We all know from the history of the Bible that this land was very good land flowing with milk and honey. As we climb this divine ladder of inheritance step-by-step, all our material blessings will be ours to the glory of the Lord in the name of Jesus.

> "Blessed be the God and Father of our Lord Jesus Christ who according to His abundant mercy has begotten us again to a living hope through the resurrection of Jesus Christ from

the dead, to an inheritance incorruptible and undefiled and that does not fade away, reserved in heaven for you, who are kept by the power of God through faith for salvation ready to be revealed in the last time" (1 Peter 1:3-4).

This is to let us know that not only do we have material inheritances here already on earth, but we also have spiritual inheritances reserved in heaven for us as God's redeemed, and that God Himself will keep us by faith to be able to get to heaven to inherit our inheritances. Praise the Lord! Alleluia.

43
Divine Ladder of Encouragement

The act of encouraging is encouragement. The word 'encourage' simply means; to stimulate progress, strength, courage, wellbeing and confidence by assisting. This assistance can be either through spoken words, prayer or deeds or all put together. We all at some point in our lives would have needed one form of encouragement or the other.

From my own personal life experiences, an encourager must be someone who can encourage himself first. As the saying goes you cannot give what you don't have. Step-by-step climbing the divine ladder of encouragement puts you in a place where you receive encouragement for yourself from the Lord, so that you will be able to encourage those around you.

"And David was greatly distressed; for the people spake of stoning him, because the soul of all the people was grieved, every man for his sons and for his daughters: but David encouraged himself in the LORD his God" (1 Samuel 30:6) KJV.

After David had encouraged himself in the Lord, he was now able to gather some of his men to pursue their enemies to recover what had been stolen from them and the Bible tells us that all was recovered in full.

"So David recovered all that the Amalekites had carried away, and David rescued his two wives. And nothing of theirs was lacking, either small or great, sons or daughters, spoil or anything which they had taken from them; David recovered all" (1 Samuel 30:18-19).

Climbing this divine ladder of encouragement by God's grace helps us not to give up in times of difficulty both in our lives and our ministries. It also puts us in a place where we can encourage fellow Christians and those around us to fulfil their goals and destiny in life. This encouragement should also extend to our parents and leaders in ministry.

"And Joses, who was also named Barnabas by the apostles (which is translated Son of Encouragement), a Levite of the country of Cyprus, having a land, sold it, and brought the money and laid it at the apostles' feet" (Acts 4:36-37).

This is quite an interesting piece of information about Joses whose name also means Joseph and whom the apostles named Barnabas (Son of Encouragement) because he was I believe always encouraging them in the work of ministry with his words and deeds. This is to let you know that we all need encouragement in what we are doing irrespective of our age, position or status.

To take this point further let's look at Jesus also in the Garden of Gethsemane in (Luke 22:42-43):

> "Saying, 'Father if it is Your will, take this cup away from Me; nevertheless not My will, but Yours, be done.' Then an angel appeared to Him from heaven, strengthening Him."

This strengthening of Jesus I think would have encouraged Him to face the cross.

44
Divine Ladder of Revelation

The word 'revelation' appears in the Bible 15 times and the word 'reveal' 12 times. The word 'revelation' means; to disclose or unveil a reality or an event which was not formerly known or seen. It can also mean to uncover or bring to light something hidden. From God's perspective what is being revealed can be something that happened in the past, can be in the present or in the future.

The book of Revelation in the Bible is a book I love so much and the Lord helps me to read it at least once every year of my life now. I read it and study it in detail asking the Lord to please teach me and show me things that are yet to happen in the future and to give me understanding.

I must say that at the centre of the book of Revelation in the Bible is our Lord and Saviour Jesus Christ. There is a divine ladder of revelation which I believe we can climb step-by-step with the help of the Holy Spirit and by God's grace, where God will be revealing to us secrets from His word and how it concerns us and mankind in general.

Revelation helps us as God's children to prepare for events that are about to unfold either in the now or the future. It also helps us to understand events that have happened in the past that have been documented in the Bible, which is God's written manual to mankind. As we climb this divine ladder of revelation, the Holy Spirit of God helps us to understand the mysteries of God and how we can appropriate these mysteries to the things of God's kingdom. It also helps us to prepare for the second coming of our Lord and Saviour Jesus Christ and to occupy till He comes.

In addition, it gives us an understanding of what God expects from us based on what He is set to do. It also keeps us busy for the Lord in all areas of ministry, especially in the area of winning souls for Him.

Let's look at what Jesus said in two places of Scriptures:

"All things have been delivered to Me by My Father, and no one knows who the Son is except the Father, and who the Father is except the Son, and the one to whom the Son wills to reveal Him" (Luke 10:22).

"So I said, Who are You, Lord?' And He said, 'I am Jesus, whom you are persecuting. But rise and stand on your feet; for I have appeared to you for this purpose, to make you a minister and a witness both of the things which you have seen and of the things which I will yet reveal to you" (Acts 26:15-16).

Here we see Jesus at the centre of revelation through the Holy Spirit. I personally think it is very important for every single follower of Jesus to have a personal revelation of Him, because it changes the way we will perceive and see Him.

Remember your personal encounter with the Lord makes Him very real to you as an individual and while the testimonies and experiences which you have heard from other people might fade away in times of adversity, your own personal revelation will stay with you because it is personal.

I have had a very personal revelation of Jesus in which we had a *'very short discussion'* and this experience is ever fresh with me even though it happened in the year 1997; I'm writing this book in the year 2014. I have had several experiences with the Lord since 1997, but that year stands out.

I must say that a very important way through, which God reveals Himself to us is through His Word, when He gives us a very deep understanding of His written word by His Holy Spirit, who as the best Teacher reveals God's mysteries to us. The more we spend time in studying God's word, the more the Holy Spirit comes to reveal the mysteries of God's word to us and we step-by-step climb higher and higher the divine ladder of revelation. This enables the Holy Spirit to teach and make us understand things that no man will teach us or talk to us about. I must say that to the glory of the Lord, there are a good number of things about God that have come to me through personal revelations and teachings of the Holy Spirit.

> "But I make known to you, brethren that the gospel which was preached by me is not according to man, For I neither received it from man nor was I taught it, but it came through the revelation of Jesus Christ" (Galatians 1:11-12).

These are the sayings of the Apostle Paul who was a man of revelations from God, we can also be the same by believing God and desiring to have revelations from him.

45
Divine Ladder of Help
꙰꙰꙰꙰꙰

The word 'help' simply means; "to offer assistance in order to accomplish a task or a purpose, to save, to rescue, to facilitate, to send in relief, to make things easier or less difficult, to contribute means or strength to such a task or purpose." Dictionary.com.

The person who renders help is called a helper. The word 'help' appears in the Bible 137 times, while the word 'helper' appears 16 times.

As we climb the divine ladder of help step-by-step, we are putting ourselves in a place where the Almighty God can help us and send help to us. My prayer is that whenever you and I need help, the Almighty God will send us help in the name of Jesus. A lot of people on earth have not been able to accomplish certain things mainly because they didn't get help.

Remember that Joseph in the Bible was remembered by the butler through the help of God, when he mentioned the name of Joseph to Pharaoh. He revealed what God did through Joseph, while he and the baker were in the prison with him, and how Joseph helped to interpret their dreams, which happened exactly how God had revealed them to Joseph. God also used Joseph to help Pharaoh solve the mystery of the dreams he had and this led to him becoming Prime Minister in Egypt. Please read Genesis chapters 40 and 41 in the Bible.

You and I as human beings on earth are going to be needing help at one point or the other in our lives which can come directly from The Almighty God or indirectly from God sending someone to help.

"I will lift up my eyes to the hills-from whence comes my help? My help comes from the LORD, Who made heaven and earth" (Psalm 121:1-2).

"From there He arose and went to the region of Tyre and Sidon. And He entered a house and wanted no one to know it, but He could not be hidden. For a woman whose young daughter had an unclean spirit heard about Him, and she came and fell at His feet.

The woman was a Greek, a Syro-Phoenician by birth, and she kept asking Him to cast the demon out of her daughter. But Jesus said to her, "Let the children be filled first, for it is not good to take the children's bread and throw it to the little dogs." And she answered and said to Him, Yes Lord, yet even the little dogs under the table eat from the children's crumbs. Then He said to her,

"For this saying go your way; the demon has gone out of your daughter." And when she had come to her house, she found the demon gone out, and her daughter on the bed." – Mark 7:24-30

"But the Helper, the Holy Spirit whom the Father will send in My name, He will teach you all things, and bring to your remembrance all things that I said to you" (John 14:26).

So from the above scriptural references we see God the Father, God the Son, God the Holy Spirit and man (empowered by God) helping people. May you never lack help when you need it in Jesus name. Amen.

46
Divine Ladder of Hope

The word 'hope' means; looking forward to an expectation happening with confidence. It is confidence in God's word that (what) He has said, He is more than able to do. Hope is always based on something so as God's children our hope is in God and His word. The word 'hope' appears in the Bible 142 times. Let's take a closer look at the following Scriptures:

> "Behold the eye of the LORD is on those who fear Him, On those who hope in His mercy, To deliver their soul from death, And to keep them alive in famine" (Psalm 33:18–19).

> "I wait for the LORD, my soul waits, And in His word I do hope" (Psalm 130:5).

> "Who, contrary to hope, in hope believed, so that he became the father of many nations, according to what was spoken, "So shall your descendants be" (Romans 4:18).

> "But Christ as a Son over His own house, whose house we are if we hold fast the confidence and the rejoicing of the hope firm to the end" (Hebrews 3:6).

Hope in God will always lead to faith in God because faith is about action. So I can say that if any one doesn't have faith in the word of God, they probably don't have any hope either that anything good is coming their way, so they just sit down doing nothing based on the word of God.

I do travel at times and before leaving my home, I will tell my contact in the place, that I'm coming, my flight details and expected time of arrival. And to the glory of the Lord my contact is always at the airport expecting my arrival. He doesn't wait for me to get to the destination first, ring and then move to the airport. This is what hope means.

There is a divine ladder of Hope in God that we can step-by-step climb daily, with our hearts filled with confidence that the Almighty God will meet and perfect all our hopes based on His written word in the name of Jesus. Hope in God keeps us alive and vibrant for Him.

> "Let your hopes, not your hurts, shape your future" – *Robert H. Schuller*.

47
Divine Ladder of Healing

This is another divine ladder we need to climb step-by-step pertaining to healing. The word 'healing' appears in the Bible 15 times, and the word 'heal' appears 46 times. I want to look at healing from the perspective of making man whole, spirit, soul and body.

To heal simply means; to restore to health and make free from sickness and disease in the spirit, soul and body.

Many times when we think of people being sick we tend to focus mainly on the body alone, but I believe that people can be sick in the spirit and soul also, which can even be more dangerous and difficult to recognise. Once man generally is sound in his spirit and soul, he tends to be well also in his body.

Let's take a look at a Scripture that talks about Jesus healing man completely, spirit, soul and body.

> "The Spirit of the LORD is upon Me, Because He has anointed Me To preach the gospel to the poor, He has sent Me to heal the broken hearted, To proclaim liberty to the captives And the recovery of sight to the blind, To set at liberty those who are oppressed; To proclaim the acceptable year of the LORD" (Luke 4:18).

This Scripture in a nutshell summarises the ministry of Jesus as it pertains to Him bringing salvation to mankind. Salvation through Christ Jesus is about total deliverance from sin and it's penalty, sickness, disease, poverty and all forms of losses and destructions both seen and unseen.

The ministry of Jesus is filled with Him healing the sick. For example:

> "And suddenly, a woman who had a flow of blood for twelve years came from behind and touched the hem of

His garment. For she said to herself, 'If only I may touch His garment, I shall be made well.' But Jesus turned around, and when He saw her He said, "Be of good cheer, daughter, your faith has made you well." And the woman was made well from that hour" (Matthew 9:20-22).

Another interesting thing to note, is that faith is required to receive healing from God through our Lord and Saviour Jesus Christ. Please refer to the divine ladder of faith earlier discussed in this book.

Let's take a look at another case of someone who we can say was sick in his mind.

"Then they sailed to the country of the Gadarenes, which is opposite Galilee. And when He stepped out on the land, there met Him a certain man from the city who had demons for a long time. And he wore no clothes, nor did he live in a house but in tombs.

When he saw Jesus, he cried out, fell down before Him, and with a loud voice said, 'What have I to do with You, Jesus Son of the Most High God? I beg You, do not torment me! For He had commanded the unclean spirit to come out of the man. For it had often seized him, and he was kept under guard, bound with chains and shackles; and he broke the bonds and was driven by the demon into the wilderness.

Jesus asked him, saying "What is your name?" And he said 'Legion,' because many demons had entered him.

And they begged Him that He would not command them to go out into the abyss. Now a herd of many swine was feeding there on the mountain. So they begged Him that He would permit them to enter them. And He permitted them.

Then the demons went out of the man and entered the swine, and the herd ran violently down the steep place into the lake and drowned. When those who fed them saw what had happened, they fled and told it in the city and in the country.

Then they went out to see what had happened, and came to Jesus, and found the man from whom the demons had departed, sitting at the feet of Jesus, clothed and in his right mind. And they were afraid.

They also who had seen it told them by what means he who had been demon-possessed was healed.' – Like 8:26-36

We can see that the Bible says, in the last verse above that the demon-possessed man was healed. There is a divine ladder of healing that as many of God's children who are sick can begin to climb step-by-step to come out of sickness and diseases.

48
Divine Ladder of Health
❁❦❧❁❦❧❁

There is a divine ladder of health, which l believe God's children can step-by-step climb with the help and grace of God. Health can be said to mean; the state of being filled with vitality and vigour with no sickness or disease in the spirit, soul and body.

Divine health simply means health from God with the above state. With divine health we are talking about the individual not falling sick at all. I believe this is very possible with God being on our side. (Luke 1:37), says:

"For with God nothing will be impossible".

I personally believe that Jesus while on earth as a man lived in a state of divine health. I have heard testimonies of some people who have for between 10 to 20 years not fallen sick or needed a doctor. I believe we need to all ask God to give us divine health which will enable us to focus more on His service and worship.

I pray you and I will begin to climb this divine ladder today in the name of Jesus. Amen.

49
Divine Ladder of Transformation of the Mind
꒦Ꙝ꒦Ꙝ꒦Ꙝ

The word 'transform' simply means; to change in form, condition, appearance, nature, structure and character. Please refer to my other book entitled: *The Mind - Battleground for Change* for a deeper understanding of the transformation of the mind. Step-by-step climbing this divine ladder helps us to come out of our old-self and ways of thinking into fully being the new man we now are in Christ Jesus in our minds.

I'm talking about us being transformed by the renewing of our minds with the **Word of God**.

If we want to be honest with ourselves, there are so many Christians in our churches today who still behave like people who haven't had an encounter with Jesus, simply because their minds are not being renewed. I'm not being judgemental by saying this or condemning, but I think it is a dangerous thing when God's children are not changing from their old sinful ways and attitudes despite the fact that they will say they have encountered Jesus for the past 20 years. Yes, change can be very gradual and slow but nonetheless there must be change from the old-self to the new person in Christ. (Romans 12:1-2), says:

> "And so, dear brothers and sisters, I plead with you to give your bodies to God because of all He has done for you. Let them be a living and holy sacrifice—the kind He

will find acceptable. This is truly the way to worship Him. Don't copy the behaviour and customs of this world, but let God transform you into a new person by changing the way you think. Then you will learn to know God's will for you, which is good and pleasing and perfect." (NLT)

As it is highlighted in the above Scripture, it is clear that without us changing the way we think and do things from our former ways, it is almost impossible to please God. A lot of Christians are still being guided by traditions in their thoughts and character, I do wonder how they intend to please God.

As we climb this divine ladder with the help of God, we start to think like God, talk like God and also act like Him.

This I believe is very possible as a gradual process coming out of the old way of thinking into the new way which is God's way. We need to remind ourselves that heaven is a place for people who are thinking like the Almighty God.

New Spirit Filled Bible says: The mind constitutes the intellect or understanding, but also includes all that is described in the word 'Mind—set,' that is, the feelings and the will. Being transformed by the renewal of the mind indicates a literal change in the form or formulas of thought or being. This describes redemption's provision of power to instil godliness in us – a power that transforms 1) Our thoughts, which lead to formulating 2) our purposes, which proceed to dictate our actions; and thus

3) our actions become character – determining habits, shaping the life and setting the course for the future.

The Bible in Proverbs 23:7a says: "For as he thinks in his heart, so is he."

The word 'heart' used here, I believe is talking about the mind of a man since the mind is the thinking faculty of a man.

"Let this mind be in you which was also in Christ Jesus" (Philippians 2:5).

The only way we can have the mind of Christ Jesus is to allow God's word to transform our minds so that we can think like Jesus and also act like Him. So as we step-by-step climb the divine ladder of transformation of the mind daily, God by His grace will make this change possible for us in the name of Jesus. Amen.

"For with God nothing will be impossible" (Luke 1:37).

50
Divine Ladder of Destiny
✄⌘∽⌘✄⌘✄⌘∽⌘✄

I want to define this word destiny from the perspective of a Christian. It can be said to mean; God's divine plan or purpose for a person on earth. So we are looking at the person living his or her life under the divinely predetermined arrangement and purpose of God.

The word 'destiny' appears in the Bible just once and the word 'destined' appears twice. Despite this, the Bible is a book that has revealed unto us the destinies of so many people and the destined end of mankind. Jesus our Lord and Saviour as a man lived a destined life on earth and He fulfilled all that the Almighty God had divinely planned for Him.

> "All who dwell on earth will worship him, whose names have not been written in the Book of Life of the Lamb slain from the foundation of the world" (Revelations 13:8).

We see in the destiny of Jesus that even before he physically came to die for man, that the Almighty God before he created the world and before man fell had already worked out a solution for man's sin. There is a divine ladder of destiny for those of us ordained by God that we need to climb daily step-by-step so as to fulfil our destiny in the Lord God Almighty.

One thing to bear in mind about destiny is that people often miss is that we have to co-operate with God to make our destiny come to pass. Even in the case of Jesus in the garden of Gethsemane, He had to co-operate with the Father in order to fulfil His destiny as the Saviour of mankind.

> "Then Jesus came with them to a place called Gethsemane, and said to the disciples, "Sit while 1 go and pray over there." And He took with Him Peter and the two sons

of Zebedee, and He began to be sorrowful and deeply distressed.

Then He said to them, "My soul is exceedingly sorrowful, even to death. Stay here and watch with Me." He went a little farther and fell on His face, and prayed, saying "O Father, if it is possible, let this cup pass from Me; nevertheless, not as I will, but as You will."

"Again, a second time, He went away and prayed, saying, "O Father, if this cup cannot pass away from Me unless I drink it, Your will be done." – Matthew 26:36, 39-42

We see that twice between verses 36-42 of this Chapter, Jesus is faced with the option of either to surrender His will to that of His Father and to fulfil His destiny or to have His will and shift away from His destiny.

Jesus had to make a choice here and twice He chose to fulfil His God given destiny. The same is the case for every one of us we can either play our part in our God given destiny or deviate from it to fulfil something else.

My prayer is that we would climb our God given ladder of destiny and fulfil our purpose on earth in the name of Jesus.

"Her uncleanness is in her skirts; She did not consider her destiny; Therefore her collapse was awesome; She had no comforter. "O LORD, behold my affliction, For the enemy is exalted" (Lamentations 1:9).

This is exactly what happens when destiny is ignored in the Lord, the enemy takes over, and this was what happened to the city of Jerusalem when the children of God were taken over by Babylon because of their straying away from God.

> "Then Simeon blessed them, and said to Mary His mother, 'Behold, this Child is destined for the fall and rising of many in Israel, and for a sign which will be spoken against" (Luke 2:34).

Knowing very well about the life of Jesus, you will agree that He fulfilled His destiny and many have risen and fallen not just in Israel, but the entire world because of Him up until today.

51
Divine Ladder of Exchange and Transfer
✂☙❧✿❧☙✂

I want to simply look at the word 'exchange' as meaning; trading places, replacing one thing with another, putting one thing in the place of another. Now in the process of exchange as in the case of when you buy an item and you get home to find out that it is not working or functioning well and you return it for an exchange, you get a good one in the place of a bad one.

In a lot of exchanges that occur in life one side tends to be at an advantage above the other. A lot of exchanges are not equal so to speak. To transfer simply means; "to change or go or cause to change or go from one thing, person, or point to another" – *Collins English Dictionary*.

We must have heard of one person being transferred from one working office to another office entirely to perform either the same previous role or one slightly different or higher. I have called this a divine ladder of exchange and transfer because it is only the Almighty God who has the right to exchange the life of one man for another. That is the death that was meant for one person is transferred from him to somebody else. This is exactly what God did for us when He sent Jesus to die in our place, because someone had to die for the sins already committed. All the other exchanges in the Bible which were not sinful were also done by God Himself, be it life being exchanged or other things or places.

> "For I am the LORD your God, The Holy One of Israel, your saviour; I gave Egypt for your ransom, Ethiopia and Seba in your place. Since you were precious in my sight, You have been honoured, And I have loved you; therefore I will give men for you, And people for your life" (Isaiah 43:3-4).

Here the Almighty God is making an exchange of lives, keeping His children alive and in their places, the heathens are dying. The evil that was meant to come to God's children was transferred to the unbelievers. This might sound cruel but hey, this is the Lord's doing.

> "The righteous is delivered from trouble, And it comes to the wicked instead" (Proverbs 11:8).

"The wicked shall be a ransom for the righteous, And the unfaithful for the upright" (Proverbs 21:18).

As we climb this divine ladder step-by-step, God spares us from evil and it comes to the wicked instead, but as we have seen from the Scripture above we need to remain righteous before the LORD.

"A good man leaves an inheritance of moral stability and goodness to his children's children, and the wealth of the sinner finds its way eventually into the hands of the righteous, for whom it was laid up" (Proverbs 13:22) The Amplified Bible.

Here the Scripture is telling us of divine wealth transferred from the hands of the ungodly unto the righteous of the Lord.
Let's take a look at another Scripture on divine transfer:

"Now there was a long war between the house of Saul and the house of David. But David grew stronger and stronger, and the house of Saul weaker and weaker;

May God do so to Abner, and more also if I do not do for David as the LORD has sworn to him—to transfer the kingdom from the house of Saul, and set up the throne of David over Israel and over Judah, from Dan to Beersheba" (2 Samuel 3:1; 9-10).

Here we see from this Scripture the divine transfer of kingship from the house of Saul to the house of David by the Almighty God Himself and not through personal struggle.

52
Divine Ladder of Possibilities

This will be the last divine ladder to be discussed in this first book, the rest will be in the second book, which you will need to read to get the full picture of what I have to say.

Before explaining this very important divine ladder, which I believe affects a lot of things that we do even though we might not even realise it, I would like to highlight that the way we view things will affect our approach to them. What I mean by this, is that if for instance, a person views a task as impossible to be done then it will be impossible for the person. If you also view things from the perspective that with God all things are possible, as the Bible says then it will be possible no matter how difficult the task may be to accomplish.

The word 'possible' from dictionary.com, means; "that may or can be, exist, happen, be done, be used."

When we have a mind-set that things are possible with God's help, God uses us to make things happen, God uses us to get things done that people cannot imagine.

The word 'possible' appears 15 times in the Bible and it might interest you to know that they are all in the New Testament. It might also interest you to know that most of the times the word possible was used in the New Testament, they were used by our Lord and Saviour Jesus, trying to encourage us to believe in God the Father.

Let's us now take a look at some of these Scriptures

> "Jesus said to him, "If you can believe, all things are possible to him who believes" (Mark 9:23).

Jesus says: '**All things are possible to him who believes**', to him who believes that the Almighty God can do it.

> "But Jesus looked at them and said to them, "With men this is impossible, but with God all things are possible" (Matthew 19:26).

Jesus is saying here that with the Almighty God on my side and your side all things are possible to us. Amen.

> "But He said, "The things which are impossible with men are possible with God" (Luke 18:27).

I want you to think on these words of Jesus for yourself and see those dreams of yours as achievable, God being with you.

This is what this divine ladder of possibilities is all about, as you start to step-by-step climb it in the realm of the spirit by God's grace you need to change your mind-set and believe the Almighty God that you can achieve great things for Him and yourself in the name of Jesus. With the help of the God of all possibilities, we can achieve the impossible.

Think about how the Almighty God parted the Red Sea in (Exodus 14:13-31), in order to save His people. Think also about the birth of Jesus and all He did on earth during His ministry, and His death and resurrection from the dead. Think also about all the written miracles in the Bible and may be you have heard a testimony of someone that God did the impossible for, if you believe God, yours will be possible too as you start to step-by-step climb this ladder in the name of Jesus.

I had an experience in Nigeria some time ago when I ran to catch a moving vehicle. My foot slipped off the vehicle and everyone thought that I had fallen and was probably under the vehicle. But as I was falling I felt someone catching me and placing my feet back on the vehicle and to the surprise of every one, I was still on board by the time the vehicle stopped because of the shouting of people around. Praise God. Alleluia.

The following quotes on possibilities might be of interest to you:

1. "Without Faith, nothing is possible, with it, nothing is impossible" – *Mary McLeod Bethune*.
2. "Nothing is impossible, the word itself says, 'I'm possible'" – *Audrey Hepburn*.
3. "In my case, I can sincerely say that nothing is impossible…. When I was saying I want to be No. 1 of the world, and I was seven or eight years old, most of the people were laughing at me because it seems like I have one percent of chances to do that, and I've done it." – *Novak Djokovic*.

CONCLUSION

෴෴

The remaining *Divine Ladders*, which are also important for you to know about will be discussed in the second Part of this book. I urge every reader of this book to make up their minds to climb their God given ladders step-by-step. The truth is that if you don't, no one will do it for you because everyone has theirs to climb and they are individualistic, just like our personal relationship with the Lord. What we can do is to encourage one another to climb and not be weary or giving up.

I want to lastly give an opportunity to anyone reading this book who is yet to meet with Jesus or give their lives to Him, to know that you need Jesus to get to heaven where God is. I call God my Father in heaven because I have a relationship with Him through Christ Jesus who died for me so that I can be free from my sins and the consequences of sin which is eternal spiritual death. As I've written in this book, at the top of all these divine ladders *is* my Lord and Saviour Jesus. If anyone doesn't have Jesus, I don't think that person is on his or her way to heaven. John 3:16 says:

> "For God so loved the world that He gave His only begotten Son, that whosoever believes in Him should not perish but have everlasting life."

If you want to make Jesus Christ Lord and Saviour of your life right now, you can pray this simple prayer of faith:

> Lord Jesus, I believe you shed your blood and died for me on the cross so that I can be set free. I confess all my sins right now before you and I say I am sorry. And from today onward I want you to come into my heart to live and guard me in your ways and footsteps. I also ask you to please write my name in the book of life. Thank you, Lord Jesus, because you have done this for me, in Jesus' name I pray. Amen.

For those who want to rededicate their lives unto the Lord, you can pray a simple prayer for the Lord to forgive you for going astray from His presence, and ask Him to help you return to Him fully again and never to go back into the world.

As you have prayed, believe that Jesus is now in your heart. My advice is for you to look for a Bible—believing church to attend so that you can get to know Jesus more.

Welcome to the kingdom of God. God bless you abundantly.

OTHER BOOKS
BY THE AUTHOR

ɷ౭ɷ౭

Please visit Author's website to purchase other books by Author.
http://www.jima660bil.com

Lightning Source UK Ltd.
Milton Keynes UK
UKOW04f1105071115

262229UK00002B/12/P